The Way It Was
COMING TO AMERICA:
The Real Story

From a small village in Africa to the
Foundation of a potentially multi-billion dollar
Corporation in America and
How he did it!

By: Tino Adognravi

03/22/07

Warmest regards,
Tino Adogn

eibBooks.com Publishing
"eXcellence in Book Selling"
Cleveland Heights, Ohio

The Way It Was *Coming To America:* The Real Story

Copyright © 2004 by Tino Adognravi

Published by eibBooks.com
16781 Chagrin Blvd. Suite 255
Shaker Heights OH 44120, U.S.A.

All rights reserved. This book may not be reproduced in whole or in part without written permission from the publisher, except by a reviewer who may quote a brief passage in a review; nor may any part of this book be reproduced, stored in a retrieval system, or transmitted in any form or by any means, electronic, mechanical photocopying, recording, or other without written permission from publisher.

ISBN 0-9762025-0-6
Printed in the United States of America
Distributed by eibBooks.com

AFRICA

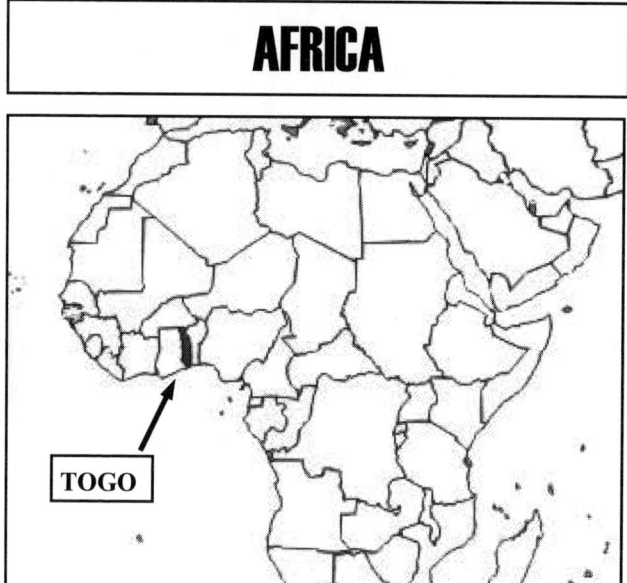

Togo is a former French colony that obtained its political independence from France in 1960. There are approximately 80 ethnic dialects spoken in Togo but the official language is French and the economy is mainly rural. The climate is tropical with rainy and dry seasons alternating throughout the year.

To My Mother.

ACKNOWLEDGEMENT

*W*elcome to The Way It Was Coming To America: The Real Story. This book has been written to share my experiences with you and with others you may think would enjoy my story. The writing style of this book is such that you get the raw effects these words were intended to convey. This book would not be possible without blessings from God and without the power of the human spirit I experienced with the American people in particular and others whose path crossed mine on my journey to where I am today. THANK YOU AMERICA AND MAY GOD CONTINUE TO BLESS AMERICA!

There are so many people that I would like to thank for giving me the opportunity to be where I am now. The list is so long that I can not list everyone here. So if you could not see your name here, it is not a statement that I did not appreciate what you have done for me. Not in any particular order: Vince Creazzo, Jim Jones, Franck Fescer, Steve Byrd, Dante Jackson, Suzanne Ruedi, Merrick Poznansky, Russell Schoe, André Missoh, Kpadé Amouzouvi, Ingrid Rewinkel, Sam Kumah, Remy Anoumou, Maurice Perkins, the Johnson family in Togo, Angèle Aguigah, Diogo Telesphore, my sisters Genevieve, Valerie, Sidonie, Marceline.

Thanks to Peggy Hill, the Golding family, Crowley-Crotser family and a special thanks to my wife Tracy the editor of this book, our children Rachelle and Daniel for hanging in there with me for the last six years while I was literally "glued" to the computer. I could not have accomplished what I did if those three people were not willing to sacrifice along with me. Last but not least, **I thank my mother** who always had a silent trust in me that I would always do the right thing. And to my father who could not give me all the material wealth of the world but told me that only my intelligence was going to take me far and I believed him.

PART ONE

From The Beginning

CHAPTER ONE

*M*y name is Tino Adognravi, born Valentin to Emanuel and Veronica Adognravi. As far as I know, I was born on Feb. 12th, 1962 in Atakpame, a small town 105 miles North of the capital city Lomé of Togo (W. Africa). Although I was the first child for my father, I was the third of five children for my mother. My two stepsisters Genevieve and Valerie are older than me and Sidonie and Marceline are younger than me. We moved back to Lomé when I was three months old.

I went to the neighborhood kindergarten school where the boys had to wear green uniforms, shorts and shirts. The girls wore white sleeveless shirts and a khaki skirt. My mother made sure that my uniform was two sizes too big so I would grow into it. I had to walk to my kindergarten school by myself everyday and due to my oversized uniform, people could tell that I was coming because my outfit made a loud noise when I walked fast. I was teased by the other kids and nicknamed kpluya the "boy with the big uniform".

Kindergarten was great and I still remember those days when the teacher would hold my hand to teach me how to form my letters. I also cherished the corn bread and boiled milk that the whole school was served once a quarter. Each kindergarten student was to bring in at least one piece of charcoal to help cook the milk and the corn bread. Typically, we had to go home in the middle of the day to eat and then return to school. On this day however, we were allowed to stay and eat the corn bread and boiled milk as a special treat.

I started first grade at the all boys St. Marie-Reine catholic school of Bè, which then was known for providing a better education than the public schools. Every morning as a child I woke up, washed up in a basin, adorned my uniform and got breakfast money from my mother. The uniform for the catholic school back then was a white short sleeved shirt and khaki shorts. The breakfast allowance was about $.25 and you could buy some rice and beans and some gari (cassava flower) and eat it before 8:45 am.

When the bell rang all the students would line up in front of the Flag Poll. The flag would be raised, the national anthem would be sung and we would march to the sound of drums played by older students.

Second grade was a great year; I had a wonderful teacher Mr. Jean. Mr. Jean was in my eyes a great teacher until he asked me to go ask my mother for a loan for him. Unfortunately when I went home and asked my mother for the loan my mother told me to go back to the school and tell Mr. Jean that she was not in the house. I went back to the school and told Mr. Jean that "my mother wanted me to tell you that she was not there." This was a bad move because I got punished by my mother and I was ignored by my teacher for the rest of the school year. He would not call on me in the classroom when I raised my hand and he would not pay attention to me at all. It was as if I were not even there.

After such a terrible year in second grade, third grade was a reprieve. I had Mr. Antoine who I considered the coolest teacher of them all. Mr. Antoine taught us the meaning of well-groomed and about the importance of the good manners. He taught us how to eat "finger food" without making a mess on ourselves by pinching the food between our thumb and index finger and extending the pinky. If I ate that way here in the U.S., I would be thought of as not being too manly. Mr. Antoine smoked a pipe in the classroom and thinking back, I can easily say that there was a pinch of a different type of herb added to his regular tobacco.

A requirement of catholic school was to go to church every Wednesday and Sunday morning. Every Monday all of the students made a big circle around the flag pole. Announcements were made and if you missed church on Sunday you were called to line up by the side of the flagpole and you were spanked. This only happened to me once and was extremely degrading. Afterwards, I decided to become an altar boy so I would never miss church again. I changed schools for my fourth grade year. My neighbor from across the street became the principal at the Public Elementary School of Nukafu. This school was near the

Airport of Lomé which was about 10 miles from our house. My mother decided it was time to have me attend that school because I would be under the direct supervision of our neighbor, Mr. Dissa and she could get a break on the annual school fees which were the equivalent of $2.00. Indeed, $2.00/year back then was a lot of money in Togo.

The extreme distance of this new school from my house meant that my younger sister Sidonie and I had to wake up around 5:30 a.m. and walk 10 miles to school. We had to stay on the school grounds during lunch. Togo has a tradition where all businesses and schools close mid-days at 12:00 and reopen at 2:30PM. This was probably due to the extreme heat of midday, and the lack of air conditioning in buildings as well as the French tradition that we inherited as part of colonization. Sometimes Sidonie and I packed our lunches and sometimes we got money to buy lunch. At times the lunch money or the packed lunch was gone after the first break period and during the lunch hour my sister and I had to go in the surrounding woods in search of Mango trees which would supply ripe Mangos for our lunch.

I spent one year at the Public Primary school in Nukafu where my teacher was Mrs. Akuvee. There were 80 students in the classroom and Mrs. Akuvee believed that the longest tree branch was the easiest way to discipline a disruptive student in the middle of the class. She could "whack" you with her long tree branch from a mile away! We had to learn our lessons by heart and be able to recite them to the rest of the class. Those who could not recite their lesson by heart had to kneel down in front of the class until each student in the class had a chance to recite the lesson.

At the end of the recitations, the students that were kneeling would choose to receive 10 strokes of a flat hardwood paddle on the tip of their fingers or on the calves (we wore shorts!) as punishment for not studying the lesson. As a result of this, a whole lot of us could recite our lessons on demand. My mother decided that staying with her and going to school in Lomé, the capital city would not be the best thing for me in the end. She believed that I would have been easily pressured by my peers to engage in negative behavior in the city. As a result, she sent me to stay with her mother in Afagna, a village 145 miles northeast of Lomé. My grandmother Anansi already had my cousin living with her. My grandmother had a small hut which consisted of a 5'x5' living room and the same size room for the bedroom. The living room also served as the kitchen where all the cooking was done by firewood. The ceiling was made out of a stack of wood and clay over which dried corn was stored for the rest of the year. The wall above the cooking fireplace was black from the smoke.

Grandma Anansi sold a traditional soap called Akoto that she made out of the ashes of some leaves mixed with caustic soda. She also sold traditional liquor called Sodabee which was made from distilled palm wine that she bought from farmers and resold Although both my parents lived in the same city, they never lived together under one roof. My mother made decisions about my schooling. That's why I ended up in the village with my grandmother. At first it felt weird to be in the village because I was a city boy that spoke Mina which was the language spoken in the capital city. Anytime I opened my mouth, people knew I was a city boy. I was the one who did not know how to hold the hoe or the hatchet to work the land. I was the one with the soft palms because I never had to do any manual work and people believed that a real man must have calluses on his hands which were a sign of hard work.

I returned to a catholic school as a result of living with my grandmother in Afagna. The catholic school was the only school near my grandmother's neighborhood. We had to go to church every Sunday otherwise we would be spanked on Monday in front of the whole school.

To avoid being embarrassed in front of the whole school on Monday, I again became an altar boy. I became one of the "boy stars" of the village and I could not miss church anymore. I was right there with the priest on the altar dressed "cool." The Italian priest that was assigned to our parish had a Volkswagen Beetle and after church in Afagna, he would take the four of us altar boys to the next village to perform the service. Sundays were the highlight of my week, as I got to interact with a male figure that paid positive attention to me. I would wash Father N.'s car with the other altar boys and he would pay us and I used my share as pocket money.

The Sunday school teacher brother André was one of the nicest men I have ever encountered. Brother André had a younger brother named Etienne who was the same age as I was. Etienne and I became good friends and he could play soccer very well. My grandmother was old and busy with her small business of selling soap and liquor. At times we would only see each other briefly in the morning. She always made sure there was food in the house for my cousin and me. I spent most of my out of school time with Etienne at brother André's house. Brother André asked me if I would like to come and stay at their house as there was enough room space for me to call home. I guess I needed a male figure in my life so I accepted that offer very fast. I moved out of my grandmother's house despite her disapproval. I was about 11 years old. Based on the fact that my life back then was between school and the church, and that brother André was known to the village people as a humble and honorable man, my grandmother could not fight my move.

Upon hearing this news my mother came from Lomé to Afagna to see what was happening. My mother came to my new home and we had a long talk in which I conveyed to her that I was happy with my move to brother André's house. After talking with brother André my mother allowed me to stay with him and Etienne.

The arrangement was that my mother would, to the best of her ability, send money and food to brother André to assist him in taking care of me. I had a weekly allowance of the equivalent of $.50. I was to manage that allowance for my breakfast at school for the whole week. On the school grounds, some entrepreneur women brought cooked food to sell to the students for breakfast. Our breakfast at school would consist of rice and beans and fried tomato sauce and fried fish. We ate the whole fish! Yes with the eyes and all. The women also served corn porridge (Akassan) or donuts and many other foods one would consider here as dinner foods. For the first time in my life I was introduced to drumming, as there was a group of kids that played drums during sermons on Sundays since no one could play the small organ we had in the church. I learned from my friends how to play the accompaniment drum and on the Sundays when I was not scheduled to serve at mass, I would play drums with other kids to accompany the church songs. These songs and drumming were jamming. I can still remember the melodies in my head now.

Because I was so involved in the church and the whole catechism deal, I found myself at times at odd with my own culture. As an adult I wish I had better wisdom back then. At catechism we learned that worshiping other Gods besides Jesus was a sin and one would go to hell by doing so. I remember, refusing to eat the food my uncles cooked after ancestral ceremonies. I was scared of committing a sin if I ate the food because the food was in celebration of my ancestors' spirits.

Afagna is a small village where, within 15 minutes walk one could walk from one end to the other; so although I was living at brother André's place I still saw my mother's people. I tried to make extra money by going to other people's farms with my extended cousins (we call that type "long sleeve cousins") where each of us would be assigned fifty square feet to hoe. When completed one would get the equivalent of $.75. I remember being laughed at because my palms got blistered from not being used to doing such hard manual work with hoes.

One memorable and difficult episode was when my fifth grade teacher asked me to deliver a love letter to the same lady brother André was supposedly dating. I was 12 years old and this was a very difficult thing for me to do because I felt very guilty about betraying brother André with whom I lived. I felt I did not have a choice about my teacher's request because I was afraid if I didn't I would be disrespecting him and would be punished.

In Afagna, the traditional workweek consisted of five consecutive days and the sixth day was for resting. The sixth day was called "Klin gbe". None of my uncles or cousins could explain the meaning of the word "Klin" to me but "gbe" means day. As I was told, no one was supposed to work on the farm on the sixth day because if one tries to do so, an accident of some sort or negative incident would happen. Wednesday and Saturdays were Market days. Wednesday was the small market day and only residents of Afagna brought to the market place their commodities to sell. Saturday on the other hand was the big market day when people from other surrounding villages within a 50 mile radius would come to Afagna to sell their commodities.

The market day started around 11:00 am and lasted sometimes up to 11:00 pm. There was no electricity and the people had to use lamps made of welded sardine cans with a piece of cloth for the wick. Kerosene was used in these lamps. Imagine having to study with this lamp while the wind is blowing and the smoke from the kerosene fills the room.

Towards the end of my 6th grade year I started showing an interest in becoming a catholic priest. When the word got to my mother she decided to get me out of Afagna. She did not want her only son to become a priest. It was expected that I would grow up, get married and provide lots of grand children. My mother wanted me out of Afagna but did not want me in Lomé the capital city because she believed the city was a bad place to be raising a boy. My mother decided to have me stay with one of her "long sleeve" relatives, Uncle Gaspar.

After my successful graduation from elementary school my mother sent me to live with Uncle Gaspar in the town of Aneho, 45 miles south of Afagna on the coast. This was far from the catholic school. I would now go to college which was the equivalent of high school in the French Educational System that Togo followed. Uncle Gaspar was 60 years old and lived with his 14 year old son and a 10 year old girl who was his maid. The setup at Uncle Gaspar's was that I would get a free room and my parents were to provide my meals. My mother would bring me food once a week and I started cooking my own meals at the age of 13.

I was accepted into the high school of Zébévee where I would study for the next three school years. Zébévee high school was about 8 miles from where Uncle Gaspar lived and we had to leave the house very early in the morning in order to make it to school before 8:45 AM. If you were late for school, you would get a whooping from the Principal or the assistant Principal. We would go to school in the morning and come home for lunch and return at 2:30. Our school days were over at 5:00PM.

One of the most embarrassing and another memorable moments in my life was my first day of high school. The plan was to have me stay with Uncle Gaspar. Unfortunately my mother and I did not leave Lomé for Aneho until that Monday morning. The trip from Lomé to Aneho was about 1 hour. We got up early on Monday and took a taxi to the bus station (actually they were pickups trucks). By the time my mother and I got to the school it was assembly time around the flagpole. The school principal was making his new school year speech and my mother told me, "Valentin go ahead, go join your school mates." My mother had a basket with my weekly food balanced on her head and as I walked toward the group of students to join in, the school principal interrupted his speech and yelled out, "Would someone tell that lady and her son to wait on the side." Everybody turned around and looked at us and some of them looked at my mother and the big basket of food on her head and started laughing. For that entire school year my peers teased me about that incident.

The town of Aneho is split in two by a lagoon with its estuary in the Atlantic Ocean. There was a single bridge that linked both sides of the town. At times we would take a canoe taxi to the big island in the middle of the lagoon and swim through the smaller side of the river to go to school. We would balance our clothes and notebooks on our heads while swimming to the other side. Once on the shore, we wiped our skin dry, put on our clothes and proceeded to the school.

It was at this high school where I was first introduced to the English language. My first English teacher was Miss Sulton, a Peace Corp Volunteer. In my classroom, we were seated on benches that would hold two students. My buddy and I chose to occupy the first bench in row 2. We thought Miss Sulton was so cute that we would not miss her class. My buddy and I were "in charge" of letting the other guys in the classroom know what color Miss Sulton's underwear was. When she sat down she did not tuck her skirt between her legs as the Togolese women are taught to do from young age. We could easily see her underwear without trying to! We learned English dialogues with Miss Sutton and the Old McDonald had a Farm song. We also learned among other things about Halloween and Trick or Treat.

In the 8th grade I joined the choir where I learned how to sing bass and tenor. In the 9th grade I started to learn how to play guitar with a classmate named Innocent who was older than me. Innocent smoked cigarettes so I paid for my guitar lessons with packs of cigarettes. One day Innocent decided he was going to introduce my buddy and me to something new (thinking back he was testing our awareness of the existence of marijuana). After having waited for Innocent to get ready to start the guitar lesson for an hour, he came out of his room and had a piece of cigarette rolling paper and a large piece of dried up leaf that looked like the leaf of a Papaya tree.

Innocent broke up the leaf, put it in the paper and rolled it up like a cigarette. He lit it, drew a couple of puffs and handed me the cigarette. I took a couple of puffs and returned it to him because it smelled nothing like a normal cigarette. We went over the guitar lesson and at the end; Innocent asked me if I felt anything after smoking the cigarette he made. I said no, he laughed and that was the end of that.

Later during the school year we had a music recital at the school. Innocent had to set up a mini band for which I was the rhythmic guitarist and he was the lead guitarist. Five minutes before the show, Innocent disappeared and when he showed up he started walking like what someone in the U.S. would call a pimp. His eyes were very red and shinny. Looking back, my buddy Innocent was getting high way before I even knew what marijuana was. During my stay with Uncle Gaspar, almost every Friday I would catch the train to Lome to visit my mother and get my weekly food supplies. On the train we had to stand on the steps of the train while the train was moving because it was so full of people, chicken and goats.

If you wanted to get to Lome in one piece you had better get on and hold on. It was considered cool to jump off the train before the train made a complete stop in the villages along the train tracks. A couple of guys lost their legs doing that, but we still did it anyway for the thrill of it. At the end of 8th grade my buddy Didier who lived on the other side of the lagoon asked his father if I could come to live with them. Didier's dad saw that I had to walk all the way across the bridge to go to school and felt sorry for me. He agreed to Didier's request and I had to spend my 9th grade school year with Didier's family.

During my stay at the Didier's I had the opportunity to meet Ms. Ingrid Rewinkel, a German lady that lived in our neighborhood who was a member of the German volunteer group that was helping the Togolese health department eradicate leprosy. We would pump water into Ms Rewinkel's water tank for money. She would take Didier and I on the weekend to the beach with her other German Friends. When she was leaving Togo for Germany, as a gift to us she registered us at the Goethe Institute in Lomé so Didier and I could study German.

Throughout my high school years in Aneho, I always came back to Lomé for summer vacations. I stayed at my mother's house even though my father lived in the same city. My father had a road construction job out of town and when the construction work was over he came to town with a second wife, my stepmother. My mother could not get over that and she and my stepmother never got along even though polygamy was accepted in our culture. When my father came over to my mother's place to discuss children issues, they would lean their backs against the wall and talk to each other without even looking at each other. I never saw them be openly affectionate with each other. I did not know how much financial help my mother got from my father but I know that we always had to struggle to pay the rent. My four sisters, my mother and I lived in a one-room house that was about 6'x 6' big.

My mother sold everything you can think of, from simple donuts, corn and vegetables to charcoal. Everything was normal in its own way until I experienced domestic violence for the first time. Genevieve and Valerie were my two older stepsisters. Their father was a land surveyor who, when his work brought him to my mother's village Afagna, even though he already had four wives, decided to marry my mother as well. He brought my mother to the city and they had my two stepsisters. But because my mother was from a village, not a city woman, the other city wives of this man never allowed my mother and her children to feel at home. In other words my mother and her two daughters were ostracized and treated badly by her co-wives. She eventually left that condition and went to live by herself. She eventually met my father, they got married the traditional way and I was born. I remember having seen my stepsisters' father twice. He was known for being a mean man, and all of his children had this inexplicable fear of him.

When my sister Genevieve graduated from elementary school and was accepted at the high school of Vogan a small city North of Lake Togo, her father came with his pickup truck to drive her to Vogan where she was to rent an apartment and attend high school. Somehow my father (who never lived in the same house with us) came by the house. He found out what was going on and he became enraged. My father rushed into our room and started throwing my mother's belongings out through the door and saying that my mother might as well follow my stepsister and her father.

My father's argument was that, for all these years he was helping raise my two stepsisters without their father's help and now that Genevieve was old enough to leave the house for high school her real father showed up to take her and no one had bothered to inform him. As my father continued throwing stuff out the door, my mother, my sisters and I stood on the side and cried helplessly. The whole neighborhood gathered around our house to see the drama. It was very embarrassing and humiliating. Even today the picture of my mother's belongings being thrown out of the house has never left my mind.

CHAPTER TWO

*M*y summers were spent with my two best friends Eddy and Edu, two boys who lived on the same block as I did. Edu and his younger brother Eku lived with their uncle. Their father was very wealthy and did a lot of traveling to Europe and the United States for business. Edu's father had a lot of wives because of his wealth. Edu's mother, who was from Ghana, left her two children with their father because of the emotional abuse she was subjected to from her brother in-law. I heard she left and went to Chicago in America.

Eddy came from a large family where his sisters, who had not attended school, had succeeded in international trade. These women went to Nigeria, would purchase all kinds of commodities, and then ship them to Togo where they would redistribute them. They made a lot of money doing this and would hire their brother Eddy as their accountant because he was going to high school and was a good mathematician. Eddy was subsequently able to learn the tricks of international trade. In the 1980s, at a young age, he started his own import business along with his sisters.

Edu, Eddy and I were 3 close friends growing up in Togo. My mother sold charcoal during this time and we lived in a shack made out of woven palm tree branches on a vacant lot in the neighborhood. Edu and Eddy went to the private catholic high school and I went to the public high school. By the 11th grade they went to France to continue their education. As teenagers, we all wanted to go to France. Those who managed to go to France came back to the country had better jobs and brought back their French wives. Before my friends went to France, the three of us made a plan. We agreed that once they got to France they would send me a letter of invitation which would enable me to get a Visa to go to France. As Edu and his younger brother got older the need to meet their mother grew. Edu sent me a letter from France telling me that he was able to find out which village his mother was originally from and asked me if I would go to the village and attempt to find his mother's address in America. The only thing they knew of their mother was her name. They also had an old photograph of her. As a kid who loved adventure, I set out to find the address of Ms Lastina. One morning I borrowed the bicycle from my neighbor's son. The bicycle had no brakes and one of the pedals was missing. I rode the bicycle with no brakes wearing only flip-flops for 125 miles to get to the village. The hardest part was going down steep hills with no-brakes and using my flip-flops as brakes. When I made it to the village, I told the people that I came across that I was looking for the family with the same last name as Ms. Lastina. They finally escorted me to this old man who was supposed to be Ms. Lastina's uncle. I explained to him the purpose of my visit and he was impressed by my good heart. He told me that he did not have Ms Lastina's address in Chicago but his other nephews in Ghana might have. He gave me the name of the town in Ghana where the other nephew with Ms. Lastina's Chicago address lived.

Now we were talking about another country, which was an English Speaking country. I spoke a little bit of English from having gone to High school but I was not going to allow that deter me from providing the opportunity for my friend to meet his mother. Edu and I concluded via correspondence that I would go on a trip to Ghana to find his mother's Chicago address. The goal was to find Ms Lastina's Chicago information so that Edu could contact his mother and go meet the mother in the U.S.

Edu sent me $20.00 from France in the form of an International Money Order. I made the currency exchange and set out to Kofroedua, Ghana, which was about 200 miles northwest of Lome, where I lived. I was an independent child and my sisters and I did not have a whole lot in common, and my mother simply made sure we had food and shelter. My father was not there because he was living with my stepmother and their children. I got up very early in the morning and did not tell my mother where I was going that day. She never knew where I went anyway, as she trusted that I would be good no matter where I went. I walked about five miles to the border between Togo and Ghana. I went through customs without a problem as I was only

17 and did not require an ID card at that point. I got to the truck station where station wagons, minibuses and school-bus-like trucks took people to different destinations. I asked for help to find the trucks that were going to Kofroedua. I remembered to exchange my cfa currency into the Ghanaian Cedis. The ride I got on was a school bus packed with people and all kinds of things, from goats to chicken.

The trip took longer than I anticipated and when I got to the village-town, I had to rely on strangers for directions to Mr. Kouma Atsu, the younger brother of Ms Lastina. There was no such thing as an address or telephone number to call for most people who lived in village-towns. I was tired and hungry and was not sure how long the money would last me in Ghana considering I did not truly understand the currency value.

Finally two young men on bicycles stopped to help me with directions to Mr. Kouma Atsu. The young men decided they could escort me to Mr. Atsu who they happened to know. The weather was hot and humid. I needed to save as much of the money as I could to make sure I could make it back home. I was certain that once I reached Mr. Atsu, he would feed me, as the custom requires him to do for a guest that has traveled many miles to see him. I thought I could make this trip and be back home the same day.

We did not have a MapQuest back then, so you'd better know your destination or you had to rely on the "cab driver" to assist you with your directions etc. The two young men took me to a house; we entered the living room and they offered me a seat to make myself comfortable. I asked them for some water and was given a cup of water. The young men asked me why I was looking for Mr. Kouma Atsu. I made sure I told them that I was being a good Samaritan by trying to help my friend who was in Europe meet his mother for the first time. We spoke Ewe, which is the language spoken in southwest Togo, and Southeast Ghana. As these young men thought I did not speak English, one of them picked up the phone in the living room and called the police on me. They were explaining to the police dispatcher that there was a young man from Togo asking around for Mr. Kouma Atsu and that they (the two young men) had me in their custody. They asked if the officer needed them to escort me to the police station. Even though they called the police on me, I was not worried.

I was comforted as I knew my mission was a noble one and getting the police involved would help my cause. I later found out that I was being detained by these young men because a week prior to my visit mercenaries had come into Ghana, supposedly from Togo, and attempted to overthrow the Ghanaian government. Since I was young and from Togo, I fit the profile of the potential mercenaries. I was very scared and did not know what I would do if these people wanted to lock me up. Good thing for me, my limited English came handy to help me understand what was going on. They finally took me to Mr. Atsu's house where I had to quickly explain the purpose of my trip to convey to them that I needed for them to trust me. Anyone who listened to the reason behind my trip would have given me a hug if we were in the U.S. I was actually very impressed by the directions the old man in Togo had given me. He was so accurate that I was actually going to meet Mr. Atsu. It is a custom that when visiting a person from out of town you buy bread to offer your host. I bought some bread for Mr. Atsu's family.

I could tell that Mr. Atsu was a bit skeptical about meeting me. His skepticism could be due to the fact that I was escorted in by the two young men, and the whole situation of the mercenaries prior to my arrival. It was getting late and I knew I should have told my mother about the trip. It was late in the evening and there was no way I would be going home to Togo that night. It became obvious that I was to spend the night at Mr. Atsu's. A perfect stranger ended up at his front door and he had to offer me a place to spend the night.

Mr. Atsu had his wife cook dinner that they shared with me and they prepared the couch in the living room for me to sleep on. I could tell they were nervous about the whole situation because they made sure they left the electric light on in the living room as if someone's duty was to watch over me throughout the night. I had so much confidence in the nobility of my mission that any unfortunate thing that could happen to me did not really matter. I loved my friend and was ready to die if my death would help him meet his mother. Somehow I had faith that everything would be alright. I could not quite sleep that night, as the couch was uncomfortable and I was concerned about my mother worrying about my whereabouts.

My mother did not have electricity nor a telephone. The next morning, I woke up to the noise of the women of the compound doing their morning house cleaning routines. I was given breakfast which consisted of corn meal porridge and I was grateful. Mr. Atsu greeted me and asked me how my night was. He opened a bible that he was holding and pulled from the pages a folded up yellowish paper. He handed me a pen and a sheet of paper to take notes. I could not believe I was going to solve a twenty-five year mystery. My heart started to pound hard. Mr. Atsu realized that I was crying and he thanked me for my courage to have taken it upon myself to help my friend find his mother. He slowly said the phone number to me, (312) 901-xxxx. I had no idea what all these numbers meant or if they were the real phone number. But Mr. Atsu's demeanor appeared as if he had just shared with me a big secret. I made sure I got the phone numbers correct and thanked him on behalf of my friend Edu, his nephew whom he had never met. Now that the mission was accomplished, I had to remember to do everything backwards in order to get back to Togo without getting lost. At that point NOTHING could worry me.

I had accomplished my mission by getting what I came to Ghana for. I took the Traw-Traw yellow school bus again. I made sure I told the driver where I was going and due to my funny French accent tainted English; they were delighted to help me get off the bus at the right places. A couple of days after my return from Kofroedua, Ghana, I sent Ms. Lastina's phone number by mail to her son Edu in Toulouse, France. When he received the letter, he attempted to telephone his mother and for the first time in his life he spoke to his mother. Edu wrote me back in Togo to thank me and also to inform me that the initial communication with his mother was a positive one and that they both cried for a long time. His mother said that she would like to keep the line of communication open. I felt a big relief and a sense of accomplishment. Edu was in France, his younger brother Eku stayed in Togo. Time passed and communication between Edu and I became non-existent as it became clear to me that my two friends Edu and Eddy were not going to send me a formal invitation to join them in France.

eibBooks.com
As in Electronic Instant Books
As in eXcellence In Book Selling

Get your book published online instantly, electronically and/or in paperback format like this book and sell it directly on Zongo*Me*.com

We show you how!

CHAPTER THREE

I focused on my education and graduated with a high school Baccalaureate to attend the only University we had in the Country. During my senior year, I was the student leader at my high school. During that same year, all the student leaders across the country were invited to a political seminar where guest's speakers from the government introduced us to the concept of leadership and the ideology of the single ruling political party of the time. My participation in that seminar was a key factor to my ability to attend the University.

Considering my family situation, there was no way I would have been able to afford room and board on the campus and the college tuition. At the beginning of the school year, I ran into one of the student leaders who hung out with me during the above-mentioned government sponsored political seminar. He told me that they were compiling a list of all the student leaders that successfully graduated from high school to submit to the student affairs administration to petition for assistance with room and board. I asked him to please include me on the list. Surprisingly, I heard that the students' affairs office had taken into consideration the fact that we were student leaders in our final year of high school and we were offered free room and board for the first two school years of college provided that we successfully passed the exams to move onto the third year of college.

The French education system which our education system was based on, allowed for three years of undergraduate studies and one extra year, plus the writing of the thesis paper for the Master's Degree. We did not have any student counseling as far as what to major in. You chose your major according to the subjects in which you had the highest scores from the high school graduation exam. Because I wanted to become a businessman like Edu's father, I decided to major in Business. With room and board taken care of, I had to pay about $50.00/year for tuition as the government subsidizes higher education provided the student passes the rigorous high school graduation exam. My mother wanted her only son to become an elementary school teacher like my cousin did when he graduated from high school. My cousin became a teacher and was able to buy a piece of land to build a house and an Italian Vespa scooter.

Buying a piece of land was the sign of having made it in Togo. I got very angry with my mother upon her suggestion that I become a teacher instead of attending college. My argument was that I did not want to be a teacher and end up being sent to some remote village where I would be lost forever. I knew there was a whole world out there for me to explore. My father told me time and time again that only my intelligence would take me far and I believed him. My father would say to me on one of those moments, "Valentine, I do not have all the wealth and big houses to give but only your intelligence is going to take you far." I told my mother that the only reason I felt she wanted me to become a teacher was so I could give her a portion of that small salary teachers made in Togo. I believed that she was being selfish. I could tell my mother was heart broken to hear me talk to her like that. I knew I could do more because my father made sure I knew I was a smart young man.

Since we only had one University in the whole country, all graduating high school students who wanted to attend college had to come to the capital city to attend the same University. This meant that each year more students came to the University than there were classrooms capable of holding the ever-increasing student population on the campus. Classes were so full people had to sit in the frame-less windows, climb on trees and/or stand outside the classroom to take notes. There was no audio system in any of the classrooms and most of the times; the students in the back of the class would start making funny noises or shout obscenities to disturb the class out of their frustration of not being able to hear what the professor was saying. It was a nightmare. In my first year of business school, there were 600 students attempting to major in business management. At the year-end exam, only two students passed the final test to move to the second year of business school.

The rumor mill reported that the only female who passed the test might have slept with the professor. That rumor would not surprise any student, as all the way from high school to University it was a known fact that some teachers or professors would date their students in exchange for good grades. Not all teachers or professors of course did that but it was frequent. As a male student, you had better not try to date the prettiest girl if you wanted to progress with your education.

So I was not successful after the first year at the business school but still wanted to become a businessman. I attempted the second year of the business school with the same unfortunate outcome. The University policy was that if a student fails twice in any department, that student had to change their major or get out of college. I wanted to become a businessman so bad that when I went to the on-campus library, I discovered John Kenneth Galbrait *American Economist's* economics theory book which was only available in English. Somehow I convinced myself that if I could read this book and understood it I might be able to successfully pass my year-end exam at the business school. It was very difficult; it was like you found the secret to open the door to the treasure chess but the secret was in a different language. All the graphs that my professors drew on the black board during class were in Galbraith's book and even better, but Galbraith's book was in English. I tried hard but I could not decipher the language and use the book as a resource. At times I felt that if I just stuck to this book, somehow all that knowledge would eventually become part of me. So I tried and tried and at times I was discouraged.

Other times I was proud of myself because of my will to acquire the knowledge out of that book and that made me feel that it was not time wasted. Most of the books the professors recommended for their classes at the University were not available in the country. One had to know someone in France and have the financial means to have the books shipped from there. That's why every student had to take hand written notes straight from the professor's presentation. The third year of my University experience, I decided, I would study History and Geography. I felt that I had wasted two years of my life trying to attend business school in the worse type of conditions.

If only I could get passed the second year at any major then I could return to business school as the University policy required. So history and geography it was and thank God, I successfully pass to the second year level. I could say I was proud that I was a real student then!

Since I failed at the business school, I lost my free room and board provided by the University. Now came the hustling times. I managed to secure a room at the dorm for my second year of History but I had to pay for my own food and supplies. My older sister Genevieve had a Yamaha 50 scooter. She fell off of it twice so she gave to me to use because she was afraid to ride it. That was a blessing in disguise as this moped allowed me to go between the campus and the marketplace of Bè where my mother and two younger sisters sold their respective items every day. My mother sold charcoal, my youngest sister sold cooking spices, and the younger one sold skin care products. I would visit them twice a week to get some money for food and gasoline for my moped, eat lunch with them and go back to my dorm. Edu had a friend he met at the boarding school he attended while he was in Togo. This friend of his, whose name was Papazi, realized that I was interested in speaking English and introduced me to Appo. Appo was supposed to have knowledge about America and had a few Peace Corp friends.

When I first met Appo, I was impressed because he told me that he knew a lot about America and had a couple of US Senators and Congressmen as friends. He told me he knew how to get the address of anyone in the US and that he would eventually go to the United States to live.

I was pleased to have met Appo. He setup a time to take me to the American Cultural Center library where there were thousands of books and magazines in English and one did not have to pay to view the magazines or read the books. Best of all, the library had air-conditioning. We could even take books out if we signed up for a library card. I did signup for the library card and was able to checkout my first library books. I could take out up to four books at a time and I was very happy. I could not quite understand all I was reading but I was determined to understand this language and believed by reading books and magazines in English, I would somehow begin to understand the language better. Soon I found out that every Friday the American Cultural Center showed ABC World News Tonight with Peter Jennings, which was followed by a movie. The audience of the news show was mostly the American Peace Corp Volunteers that came down to the capital city every weekend to escape the rigors of their rural area assignments. Togolese citizens were also welcome as long as they could understand English. The first couple of times I went to see ABC News with Peter Jennings, I could only pickup a few words of what was said on screen. I thought the Americans spoke too fast and tilted their head frequently when they talked like Peter Jennings did. It was nothing like anything I heard from my English teachers I had throughout my high school years. Even Ms Sulton who was American spoke to us very slowly. But I was determined.

Friday afternoons became the highlight of my week as I did all I had to do to allow myself to be free to go watch the ABC news with Peter Jennings. If nothing else, the place was air-conditioned and watching the ABC News was like a free movie to me. To maximize the opportunity to understand American English I borrowed a friend's Walkman tape recorder and I would take it with me to the cultural center and record the news. Back on the campus, after lunch I played the recording of the Peter Jennings newscast and tried to talk as fast and as American as I could. My colleagues at the dormitory would laugh at me and they nicknamed me "Tino the crazy American". Some times my colleagues would walk pass me and say things like "Who knows, Nobody knows, God Only knows" in reference to a joke about a translator during colonization who had to translate during church when the priest said "Who know, Nobody knows, God Only knows". The translator instead translated to the people as "whose nose is it, it's nobody's nose, it's God's only nose".

In other words, my colleagues by saying that joke to me, they were telling me that with my eagerness to learn the English language, I do not end up like that mythical translator! They thought I was taking my desire to speak English to another level.

I was not discouraged and I continued recording the news and practicing my American English. I also found out that Appo the gentleman with the US senator friends did not go to school, nor did he have a job because he would visit me on campus during lunch hours and I had to feed him from the doggy bag I brought from the campus restaurant. Appo would then take a nap on my bed while I was outside practicing my English. It became clear to me that Appo had some mental problem that was not diagnosed. With my today knowledge, I would say Appo had autism.

The few times I visited Appo's house, his parents and brothers were surprised that he even had a friend that was a student at the University and who would actually come to visit him. I knew immediately by the way his family talked about him with disdain that something was up. It was kind of disappointing because after all he was the one who introduced me to the American Cultural Center which I could see clearly was changing my life. I could see what was going on in the rest of the world via ABC News and at the same time improve my English. I did not know then that Peter Jennings was a Canadian!

With the University work becoming harder and harder it became necessary for me to sever my interactions with Appo because I realized that he lied to me about a lot of things including his US Senators friends. Appo used the "Who's Who in America" book to go around and tell people that he knew specific people in the US and that so and so was going to send for him to come to America. During the 1986-summer break, I stayed at the dorm because I did not have a place to stay at my mother's. I had learned that my mother has moved behind the oil refinery in Baguida where land was free to build on as long as the building was not made of cement. If the building was not made of cement, it was made of woven coconut branches. So I stayed on the campus where we had electricity and running water. My decision to stay on the campus was reinforced by a visit to my mother's new place after I heard that she and my sisters were evicted from their previous place for non-payment of rent. The supposed new place was a shack made of woven coconut branches with pieces of rusted corrugated iron sheets as the roof. The flooring was simply dirty sand like you would see on a polluted beach. Nothing in my entire life was that depressing to me considering all the shacks we've lived in. I thought to myself there was no way I was going to live in those conditions especially after having been on the University campus where we had electricity and running water and flushing toilets; although most students from the countryside did not know one is supposed to sit on the toilet instead of squatting on it.

The biggest break of my life occurred on a Thursday evening when my roommate and I went to buy dinner on the side street near our dorm. As I was waiting to be served my Akumey (polenta and sauce dish), I saw two Caucasian ladies trying to buy a loaf of bread from a Togolese woman. I could see a lot of sign language and gestures between the three ladies. As always the "gentleman" in me got up to offer assistance for the bread buying transaction. I found out that the buyer ladies were speaking English so my Peter Jennings English came in handy.

The ladies told me they were Americans and appeared to be pleased with my English and my help. They told me that the following day was the birthday of one of them and if I could help them find a restaurant downtown that could seat a party of 20. I was invited to the birthday dinner as well. Someone actually thought I spoke good English. In fact these were two American ladies; not just some Togolese people! I felt validated in my efforts to learn English. The night could not pass quick enough for me to go find a restaurant for the party. Early the next day, I rode my Yamaha 50 moped downtown scouting out a couple of restaurants along the main boulevard in the capital city. I eventually settled on going with "Restaurant La Pirogue" (French word for **The Canoe**). I made the necessary arrangements to inform the ladies about the restaurant and the directions to get there.

I found out that these ladies were part of a group of 20 students from the University of California Los Angeles (UCLA). The group came to Togo through their UCLA's Education Abroad Program (EAP). I met the group of students and their professor on the campus and we all took the University bus to the restaurant. At the restaurant, Stephanie the birthday girl, asked me to sit next to her, as I was her guest. It was a special night for me so far. There I was, poor little guy who was living on campus because I did not have a place to stay with my own family, in the company of a bunch of Americans all speaking American English. It was like a dream come true. The menu was passed around, everyone made their selection and so did I. The jokes started flying; I had to pay close attention to keep up with the conversations and the idioms. I got some jokes; I missed some and smiled a lot. At times I did not know the subject matter of the conversation and let my mind imagine what was being discussed by reading body language and facial expressions.

My mind had to work fast because this was no ABC news with Peter Jennings; this was real Americans speaking real American English not made for TV. Dinner went pretty good. I had some fish with rice and when desert came around I passed on it. After desert the waiter returned with the bill and submitted the bill to the birthday girl. She pulled out her wallet and put some cfa bills with some change on the table, and then I saw the rest of the group pull out their wallets. They began to ask how much was their dinner selection etc. Suddenly there was a chill that came upon me. I was wondering what was going on, why did everyone take out their wallet, at a birthday party dinner? Each of the Americans was paying for what they had ordered.

You see, in Togo if I invite you for a drink, I pay for everything. When there is a birthday party, the person celebrating pays for everything. The guests are not expected to bring any gifts. So there I was with an equivalent of $.75 in my pocket and having eaten a dinner worth five dollars. I started to sweat, as I did not know what to do. I did not find any of the conversation around me interesting any longer, the big smile quickly faded from my face. I felt I was in for big time humiliation. Lucky for me I was sitting next to the birthday girl, Stephanie, who picked up on the discomfort that came upon me? Everyone put money on the tray except me. Then to my relief, she stated that because I was her guest she would pay for my dinner. Stephanie pulled out her wallet once again and paid for my dinner. I asked myself what in the world was I doing hanging out with these people? That was my first lesson in American culture 101 "**Take care of you first.**"

The birthday dinner was over and the group decided they wanted to go to a bar on the other side of town to hang out for the rest of the night. Well, now I had to decide if I wanted to continue hanging out with these people considering everyone had to pay for what they consumed. I must admit that I found hanging out with these Americans was a very enriching experience. I saw my horizons widening in front of my very eyes. I was in the middle of discussions on all kinds of things and heard jokes I'd never heard.

Heck, I wasn't going to allow being poor with only $.75 in my pocket ruin this experience for me. I decided to head to the bar with the group. I had two choices when we got to the bar, I could either not drink anything at all, or I could ask the waiter to serve me plain water in a glass which would be free of charge.

We got to the bar and the whole group sat at the big table and everyone started ordering their drinks. When it came time for me to order, I asked the waiter how much the sparkling water was and she said it was $.50. I ordered the sparkling water. It came in the same size big bottle like beer. When I was served my drink, I made sure I peeled off the sparkling water paper label, so no one realized I was only drinking water. I still had my pride to preserve! Back then, there was no pressure to push the customer to continue drinking or leave the bar, so I sipped on my bottle of water to make it last the entire time we spent at the bar.

As long as the bottle was half full, the waiter would not take it away and expose the fact that I was done drinking. So half full was my bottle of water for the entire night! Second lesson on American culture 101, some of the young beautiful women in the group were smoking cigarettes and they were not at all dressed as whores. In my culture the only women who smoked were prostitutes. Additionally, when it got later in the night, three or four people at a time would say something like "we are going to split." I asked what "split" meant, and was told that they were going back to the campus. I wondered why they were leaving the group? Why wouldn't they wait for everybody so the group could go back to the campus as they came to the bar? See, for all in my life and culture, when "We start something as a group, we finish it as a group." Splitting before the rest of the group was ready to go, was considered selfish and rude.

My second lesson was FREEDOM. American women have the same freedom to smoke cigarettes as did the men, and each person has to take care of themselves and do what they need to do and when they want and need to do it. This latter part requires personal responsibility and planning on the part of the individual. The members of the group that were splitting from the group at the bar were going to take a taxi to go back to the campus. They were going to pay for the taxi.

All my life, because of my family situation, I never had anything of value from my family because my mother did not have the luxury to provide me those things. Most of the things I had from clothing to shoes were hand-me-downs. I was the one that my peers had to chip-in to pay my way on the rare occasions I went to movies, or to the Sunday night disco. I was the one that Edu gave his father's old clothes and shoes to. Although the pants were too large, I was able to fix them with needle and thread manually so magnificently that on our outings, you would never know that they were fixed by hand. The only problem was that you would not see me sitting down with my legs spread out. I sat with my leg crossed which is considered a regal posture. I wasn't trying to be cool or anything; I simply was hiding the hand-made seams in the crotch of my pants. I did not have a choice if I wanted to fit in with my peer group on outings.

The hand-me-down dress shoes were usually a couple sizes smaller than my feet because I have big feet. I tried to stretch them out by soaking the shoes in water and putting big rocks in them with the hope that the leather would stretch so the shoe would eventually fit me. We would go places and I had to take breaks every so often to take off my shoes because the pain I felt in my feet was so excruciating to the point I could not feel my toes. I was the one that visited my friends and would not leave until late in the night because I had nowhere else to go.

Others had to share their lunches and dinners with me because I had nothing to eat. Because I was a nice young man with good manners and no means, and no knowledge of any opportunity to change my situation, people took pity on me and helped me a lot in my life and I am grateful. This inactive dependency was all I knew. Even though I started to get tired at the bar with the American students, I could not "split" and return to the campus on my own because I had no ride nor money for the taxi to get there. So I stayed at the bar embarrassingly, now that I knew what was expected of me till the last group of students decided to return to the campus and I caught a ride with them. When the taxi dropped us off, once again all the students chipped in to pay for the ride and once again it was reinforced in my mind that, self-reliance was the way it was going to be with these Americans. I got on my sister's moped which I left in front of the American students' dorm and went back to my dorm. What a night and what an experience!

The professor in charge of the students had accompanied them to the restaurant. Before he departed, early in the evening, he mentioned that he would like me to stop by the dorm the next day to meet with him. I was happy to believe that my English speaking ability enabled me to communicate with the Americans to the point that Professor P. wanted me to come back the next day. When I returned the next day professor P. asked me if I would be interested in joining the team of students on a two week trip where they would be traveling north in the country. He mentioned to me that he thought I got along pretty well with the students. I agreed and professor P. told me he would pay me $250.00 at the end of the two weeks.

Government statistics estimated that the average Togolese worker had a yearly income of $250.00. There I was, a broke student that just got offered my first job ever. In Togo there were no summer jobs for students. Those who got any type of temporary job had to know somebody in the government or someone higher up in the political system to help place them in one of the businesses. I started to realize the truth in what my father used to say to me when he said, only my intelligence would take me far. I had the opportunity to travel with the Americans for two weeks and get paid a year's salary at the end of the trip. We took the University bus to Notse, a town about 160 miles north of the capital city. In Notse, part of my job was to be the translator and cultural interpreter for the American students. Each student had a project that they had to do a field study on and write a paper on their findings. These projects ranged from the study of Notse's biweekly market sessions to the study of childhood diarrhea and its treatment among the Togolese women. The time spent during those two weeks in Notse was uneventful. There was not a job description for me per say. I only knew that I was to tag along with the students every day and be the liaison between them and the Togolese people. The sight of these young men and women created an excitement in the village-city of Notse as every morning from 9:00 AM to 3:00 PM we stormed the marketplace as a group and each student would go on his or her own to conduct their field studies.

Somehow, I realized quickly that in order to assist the American students with their projects, it was important to introduce them first to whom ever they felt they needed to interview. I would introduce the student and myself and made sure that I explained the reason why we were at the marketplace. I would say things like, "Hello madam. Here is Mike, who is a student in America and as part of his graduation exam, he needs to write a paper about how a small business such as yours is run in Africa; He came to Notse and when he saw your stall, he thought you had an interesting setup and would like to know if you would please speak with him a bit about what you do? The discussion was for Mike's use only and was not intended to be submitted to the Togolese government for any purpose what so ever."

Most of the time after going through my "spiel", the people felt at ease and would speak to us. In Togo, women dominated the small business sector. In fact, as we were growing up it was common to hear things like "a woman's destiny is to do business." What that means is that a woman ought to be able to do business because selling something was a guaranteed way to provide food for her family. Young high school girls would say things like, "I don't have to do my school homework, because I will get married anyway and run my own business."

In any case, the women at the marketplace in Notse at times would burst into laughter at the American questions. They thought the answers were obvious thus the questions were stupid. My challenge at times as translator was to tone down the brutally honest comments the Togolese women would say about the physical characteristics of the American students. Again, most of the people we had to interview had never seen a Caucasian person up close. One example of this was when we would be in the middle of a good interview and the interviewee would say things like "Goodness this one has such a big nose like an owl's beck", and they would start laughing after having said that. I had to pretend and keep a straight face and give a fake translation which went something like "she said you Americans ask some silly questions and why would anyone from as far away as America come to interview her."

A good portion of my time in Notse was also spent telling the children to go away; as they would follow us because this was the first time they had seen Caucasian people. Even for those who had seen Caucasians before, they still followed us chanting "Yovo, Yovo bonsoir, ca va bien, merci." Even most grownup Togolese people would chant the Yovo Yovo song. That quickly became annoying. I used to chant the Yovo Yovo bonsoir song when I was a kid myself because we learned that it was the thing to do once you encountered a Caucasian person. Most Togolese people today would not know what the true meaning of the term Yovo is or the chanting. Due to the fact that I was a history major, I learned that during the colonization of what is called today Togo, the French settlers forced the indigenous people to run up to them when they saw them passing by to greet them. In other words, when a farmer saw a French man coming through, the farmer had to drop everything and run up to the French guy to say hello to him.

Those who did not run up to the French men to greet him were beaten. The greeting dialog went like this: The Togolese individual would run up to the passing French man; Togolese

person: "Yevu, Yevu bonsoir" meaning (White man, White man good afternoon).
French man: "Ca va bien?" meaning (How are you doing?).
Togolese person: "Merci" meaning (Very well thank you).

    Because of the attitude of racial superiority portrayed by the French settlers and the mistreatment the Togolese people experienced during the earlier dealings with them, the Togolese people nicknamed the French Yevu as in Ye (cunning) Vu (dog). So when the Togolese ran to the European to great him so "politely" for fear of being beaten, the fact was that he was insulting him while making him feel he was being shown the sign of respect. The Togolese people made sure, either concertedly or for self-preservation purpose, not to explain the Yevu expression to the French. He just knew he was called a Yevu.

    With political independence from France, the Togolese did not have to run up to the French to greet them in that manner any longer; but the chanting continued and somehow the children seemed to be the ones that carry on that custom without even knowing the meaning. Of course once in a while you would hear a grownup chant the greeting out of excitement of seeing a white person, as if they think chanting it would please the white person as it did in the past. Linguistically the expression Yevu has evolved to Yovo, which in itself has no linguistic meaning except that it's the expression to call a white person. I could not explain that historical fact to my American students. They sure got aggravated with the chanting soon enough and some of the male students in the group said that if they could, they would have kicked some kids in the rear-end because of the constant annoying chanting and the requests by the children for money.

    Up until then, I never had a "true" girl-friend because I never had any money thus could not afford a date. As they say "proximity creates friction", and during our two week stay in the city-village of Notse, I started to like Stephanie the birthday lady, but she let me know quickly that she was not interested in me emotionally. I kind of expected to be rejected by her because I just knew I could not afford to date her. I always felt I did not stand a chance with any woman even the Togolese ones thus I never dared to ask anyone out. Our stay in Notse was uneventful except when one of the students who was an African-American got sick with Malaria and would not allow the African Doctor to treat her. She had to be transported back to Lomé, the capital city, to be treated by the Peace Corp nurse who was a white lady! This situation shocked the other Caucasian students in the group and caused some discussion for a while. The group returned to Lomé after the two weeks in Notse and was given a week of free time to explore Lomé before heading back to the U.S.

Before we got back to Lomé, we took a trip as a group to the village known as the first site where the Ewe people settled during their flee westward from the slave catchers of Yorubaland, which is today referred to as Nigeria. In this village there was a remote hut that was supposed to house the spirit of the first Ewe people's ancestors. The hut was behind two giant Iroko trees. In that hut was a beehive that was supposed to be the protector of the hut. After visiting with the traditional chief to pay him our respect and formally ask his permission to visit the village, we were taken to this hut, which is considered the shrine of the Ewe people. The Ewe people are the majority ethnic group of southern Togo. At about a hundred feet from the hut, we were told to take off our shoes, as wearing shoes would have been "disrespectful" to the spirit of the "Ancestors." From a large clay pot under the huge Iroko tree we were to cleanse ourselves by pouring water from the pot over our heads and over our feet. I took the lead and did what the old lady told us. Only an old lady took care of the shrine, as the person had to be in her post-menopausal years.

A couple of students chose not to get close to the shrine and did not have to take off their shoes and follow us to the bee-containing hut. As we went closer to the hut the old lady warned us that we were to start thinking positive thoughts and before we got too close to the hut we must let go of any grudges we had against anyone. Anyone with negative thoughts and grudges would be attacked by the bees. So the choice was clear, only the brave and the intentionally "pure" could approach the shrine. To my surprise, only three students chose not to follow the rest of the group. The old lady told us the legend of the settlement of Ewe people and how the bees saved them by producing honey that the people lived on and by chasing the slave hunters away so they never came back. The old lady told us that nowadays, the descendants of the village go to the shrine to pray to the spirit of their ancestors for assistance in dealing with life's issues like combating a disease or finding a new job. Basically the individual would make a pledge to the Ancestor's spirit by saying things like "if you (the spirit) help me find a new job, I will come back here and will buy two bottles of imported liquor and a goat to be slaughtered and cooked and share with others in celebration and gratitude for your help." The old lady told us that those who pledged and got what they wish for and who do not come back to the shrine to honor their pledge end up in more misery than they were in prior to making the pledge.

  We were asked if any of the American students would be interested in making a pledge. I knew I could not afford anything so I did not volunteer to wish for anything. In fact the wishes and pledges were silent; no one needs to hear anyone's wishes and pledges. To my surprise, Wayne, who was one of the male students, stepped forward to make a wish. To our surprise, as the old lady went inside the hut to "announce" our arrival, the bees went crazy. We were told to remain calm and that we had nothing to worry about as we took off our shoes and were supposed to have positive thoughts and no grudges.

  We returned to Notse, packed up our stuff and got back to Lome which was like going "back to the civilization" with all of the amenities which were available on the campus. My self-confidence grew and I became the go-to person for the students. I took them to my sister who was a seamstress to make them African dashikis. I became the "star" as all the other Togolese students wanted me to "hook them up" with the American girls, and they say that I could really speak this American English now in a conversational way. I just remembered when my dormitory comrades were laughing at me when I was practicing talking like Peter Jennings, now my English had come in hand y and I got paid $250.00. I told them that in order for me to introduce them to the American students, I will need to teach them American

English first and that I had to charge them for it. I made sure to charge extra for the students that I remembered were making fun of me while I was practicing talking like Peter Jennings.

    I had in all five Togolese students who wanted to learn English from me for four weeks. My private English session with them were in the evenings under a street light pole because we could not find a place to accommodate the class. It was a very funny sight to see these five guys trying desperately to make the "th" sound as in "The father"; they would say things like "V FaaVer" instead. I made in all with them about an equivalent of $25.00 all together. By the time my private Togolese English students completed their sessions with me, the UCLA students were already gone back to the United States. Two of my students got very angry that they did not have the chance to hangout with the American students before they left thus wanted their money back from me. I had to convince them that it was not my fault that the American went back to their country and that I delivered my service to them as they were able to carry on basic greeting dialogs with an accent close enough to "Peter Jennings' accent"! What a summer that was!

    I used the money earned that summer to get me some used clothes from the flee-market downtown, paid part of my rent in advance and bought school supplies.

eibBooks.com
As in Electronic Instant Books
As in eXcellence In Book Selling

Get your book published online instantly, electronically and/or in paperback format like this book and sell it directly on Zongo*Me*.com

We show you how!

CHAPTER FOUR

As I begun the school year the following September, I was energized and full of optimism. I continued going to the American cultural center every Friday to view Peter Jennings and World News Tonight. I used to love seeing President Reagan in the pressroom. When he talked I saw nothing but conviction and inspiration. That summer was so empowering that I decided to do a double major. I enrolled to major in English as well as continuing with History in Geography. I was able to study linguistics and English Literature. I was able to read and understand books on America and was able to use this knowledge in my American history classes. All of a sudden, I realized that I was not an ordinary student any longer; I knew more about what was going on in the rest of the world than the average Togolese student, and even more than some of my professors, thanks to Peter Jennings and World News Tonight.

Six months after the students departed for the U.S., I received a certified letter containing a $100.00 money order from Wayne the Caucasian male student who made a wish at the shrine in the village. In his letter to me he was pleading with me to use the money to go back to the village to buy two bottles of Whisky and give the rest of the money to the old lady. Wayne needed to do this because he had wished to be accepted on his college's basketball team. When he returned to the U.S., indeed he was accepted on the basketball team and he was the shortest Caucasian basketball player that ever made the team. So he freaked out and remembered his wish in the village.

So there I went on my sister's Yamaha moped to the village. I did as Wayne instructed me to because I did not want to be the reason why he did not honor his pledge and take the brunt of any negative consequences. The old lady was pleased to see me again and was happy about the money Wayne sent. She did a "thank you" ceremony on behalf of Wayne and I stood in for him at the shrine. On my way back to Lome, I ran into rain and there was no shelter on the side of the road to protect me from the rain. I rode the moped for about 60 miles completely drenched and almost died when I got off the moped. I was so cold my teeth were chattering. I had to put a towel the lady at the maquis (African restaurant) gave me into my mouth to prevent my teeth from shattering. I was grateful the ladies at the maquis were kind enough to take me in even though they did not know me and provided me with towels and blanket to help warm my body up. I wrote Wayne back to inform him that the mission was accomplished and never heard from him again.

I supposed Professor P. was satisfied with my role with his group because I was asked to assist another group the following summer. This time there was another professor who led the group of UCLA students. Professor S. was the leader this time and the students were older than those from the previous summer. At this time, my involvement with the American students started as soon as they came into the country. Professor S. spoke French because he was a Peace Corp volunteer in the country of Niger 10 years earlier.

The weekend following the students' arrival, I led the students to a dance club downtown. At the dance club, somehow I became attracted to one of the female students who happened to have been a Peace Corp volunteer in Benin, the country East of Togo, where she taught English in a high school three years earlier. She was on this trip as her way of returning to Africa with a chance to visit Benin once again. Togo was close enough so that at the end of the EAP program she would take a road trip to Benin to visit the friends and students she left behind when her contract with Peace Corp was over. This lady's name is Amelia. As the new group spent two weeks in Lomé learning or improving French, my role was to assist professor S. setting up the trip in the country side by arranging room and board for the entire group. I had to take couple of trips to Khalimba, a village-city 160 miles northwest of Lomé, to setup the accommodations for the group.

Romance grew very quickly between Amelia and me. I started to believe that I actually found a girlfriend and felt a sense of romance. The strange part of that young relationship was that this lady was interested in me for who I was, as I had nothing except that little Yamaha moped which belonged to my sister. I did not have a lot of clothes but always wore clean clothes with my red and white bandana given to me by one of the previous students rolled around my neck to keep sweat from ruining the collar of my shirt.

At the end of the day, I would take Amelia for a ride downtown but doing that felt awkward and I felt I was being selfish. I felt I was neglecting the rest of the group even though my official translator/guide role did not begin until we actually took the trip to Khalimba. Amelia and the rest of the group considered themselves as adults and could do anything they wanted to do at the end of the day. I had to adjust to that mentality. It had to be explained to me that although they all came on the same plane and from the same country, they did not know each other until the day of their departure from the United States, with some even meeting the rest of the group only midway to Togo. So, I did not know how to handle romance in front of others considering I never saw my father and mother hold hands or kiss. Anything else of romance was from the various Hollywood movies and the rare pornographic materials I got exposed to. I thought I knew how to French kiss but quickly learned that I did not have to stick my tongue in her mouth.

After returning to the U.S. from her Peace Corp assignment in Benin, Amelia went back to UCLA to complete her Masters degree in public health and hoped to use this trip to Africa to conduct field work from which she would write a paper for her thesis. She asked me if she could stay with me after the EAP program in order to go visit Benin. She would return to Togo where she would fly back to the U.S. Of course I said yes.

When the group got to Khalimba, as protocol, I figured it would be a good idea to go pay a visit to the political authorities in order to inform them of our visit to the town and also to brief them on the various field studies the students would be conducting for the next two weeks. First we visited the mayor of the city of Khalimba and then we went to visit the traditional chief. When we entered the chief's compound, we were to be announced to the chief and his assistants were to be summoned prior to him receiving us. I was expecting an old man in his seventies or eighties but when they escorted us to the chief's court; he was a young man of about thirty-five years of age.

We were told that he inherited his father's throne while he was a young man living in the capital city Lomé. When his father passed away six months earlier, as the eldest son, he had to assume the chieftaincy. All his assistants were old men and one could not speak directly to the chief, you had to speak through an interpreter who repeated everything to the chief even if the chief clearly could hear and understood everything you just said. As part of the protocol, that was just how it was. You did not talk directly to the chief, period! This young chief was said to have taken four wives in the six months since he had become chief. As I knew what to do, I told Professor S. that we needed to take a bottle of whiskey with us to the chief's house as well as a bottle of Gin that the chief would use for libation to bless our group for a successful stay in the town of Khalimba.

The next day we hit the marketplace where the students canvassed it and started interviewing the women merchants for their respective projects. I found out that the only African-American female student of the group has decided to change her project and chose to study what it meant to be a chief and how that impacted the relationship between the chief and his people. This village town had about three hundred thousand people. As I had to interpret the communication between this student and the chief we found out that the chief had been a mechanic in Lomé and spoke French. He could not speak French to us at the time we "officially" visited him as a group. But one-on-one he could speak French if he needed to. He decided not to have all his assistants around when dealing with us as the interviewing session continued. The second week of our stay in Khalimba, this female African-American student studying the chieftaincy sadly informed me that she had slept with the chief and now was heartbroken. She found out only after sleeping with the chief, that he had four wives and that she could not convince him to leave the chieftaincy to come to America with her. I thought at least she got her fantasy fulfilled! She slept with the African chief! I also thought about how devastated she must have felt when she realized that this man had slept with her knowing he would never leave his people to go to the US and be with her! My romance with Amelia was growing strong. I did not know how to handle that in public, as romance is a thing that happens in the dark in my culture. You rarely see two lovers holding hands on the street. Amelia wanted to display affection for me as she normally would I guess in the U.S. but I felt uncomfortable especially when professor S. was around. I felt this would be disrespectful to my boss.

    I realized later that professor S. did not really care about what the students did after hours as long as they were physically safe. Everything went on smoothly that summer and the group returned to Lome. One week later, they all returned to the U.S. except Amelia who stayed with me at my dormitory. Before Professor S. returned to the U.S., he tested my proficiency in English and wrote a recommendation letter for me on an UCLA letterhead sheet indicating his appreciation of my support to his group. He said that I was a very valuable resource and made the whole trip and experience a successful ones for him and his students. Of course he paid me my $250.00. I was happy. That letter of recommendation helped me find a job later when I came to America.

    There I was now with Amelia, the Caucasian American student, living with me. Amelia was 6 years older than I was and I was 23. I had to learn very fast about condoms and diaphragms. I took Amelia to go visit my mother and sisters in the market of Bè. I could see the relief in my mother and sister at the fact that I finally had a girlfriend, which meant I was OK physically. Little did they know that I would not date anyone because I always felt that I was not good enough and that I could not afford to take any girls out on dates? Amelia had her own money and could take care of herself and most of the times would pay for the food we ate. Early in the relationship I had a complex about dependency because she had money I did not have. She even had a couple of credit cards, and I always felt that she would think that the only reason I was with her was because of her money. The simple reality was that she had some money and I did not. The $250.00 earned over the summer went to pay for my rent, food and some used clothes and shoes for me.

Amelia had a job teaching English as a Peace Corp volunteer in the village of Aplahoe. To get to Aplahoe we would leave early in the morning, fill up the gas tank of my Yamaha 50 and head north. I made sure Amelia wore the better helmet and I wore the one that came with the moped. Wearing helmets was an ordinance in Lome at the time and people simply wore anything that looked like a helmet to avoid police harassment. The helmet I wore was too small for my head and could only be worn on the back portion of my head.

The quickest way to Aplahoe was to go north to Notse and head east to cross the border into the Republic of Benin. I had on my denim jeans and a Batakaly shirt that Amelia had given me. A Batakaly shirt is a sleeveless shirt, which is made out of woven strips of Kente cloth that has a pocket on each side. Amelia also wore denim jeans pants and a white T-shirt with a tank-top under it. She had her backpack, which contained fruit, clothes and grooming items, as we were not really sure how long the trip was going to take us. After eighty miles on the road, we ran into a thunderstorm. There were about 15 miles before we came to the next village along side the road, so we had no choice, but to tough it out as stopping the moped would not do us any good. We had no raincoats, which was a luxury back then. All of a sudden I had a dejà-vue moment and a chill rose from the lower end of my spine. It brought back the fear of death I experienced while coming back to Lomé on the same route after paying off the promise of Wayne the short basketball player.

We got to the next village and entered a small side-of-the-road bar where we were able to dry ourselves and change out clothes. We waited out the rain and resumed our journey east. We reached the eastern border of Togo around 3:00 pm. We stopped on the Togolese side custom office, greeted the officer and gave him the reason of our trip. We explained that we expected to return the same day. The officer recorded our passing through and showed us the way to the custom building on the Republic of Benin side. I greeted the officer first addressing him as "Chief". The chief was more interested in having a chat with Amelia than with me. At that point the custom officer informed me that Amelia needed a visa to enter the country. Amelia had her passport but somehow we failed to find out about the visa. I did not really know what a visa was at the time. We ended up paying 2,000 cfa (about a $4.00) to the officer to let us through. He had a big smile and let us through with good wishes.

From the border to Aplahoe we had another hour and a half on the road. Now I had no idea where I was. I was in a different country in the countryside with a Caucasian woman on my Yamaha 50. The only map we had was the Amelia's, based on the memory of people from Aplahoe coming to Togo the same way. We relied on road signs and the few farmers we passed by to find our way to Aplahoe. We finally and luckily arrived in Aplahoe around 6:00 p.m. and I realized that there was no way we could return back to Lome the same day. Right away Amelia got really excited because she could now reconnect with the small town that she called her home four years earlier. We went directly to the compound where she lived. The women screamed and jumped from joy and excitement at the sight of her. After hugs between Amelia and the women and their children were exchanged, we took off to go find an old friend of hers. Luckily we found Mr. Amoujou who by the way had six wives and 25 children. As the excitement went on, we needed to decide where we were going to spend the night. Mr. Amoujou offered us to spend the night at his place and we were grateful. The next day we left Amoujou's place and went to the small hotel in town that was still in business. We got to the motel around 9:00 pm. I did not know how much money Amelia had and could afford but I just knew she had some money as I did not and I would not have come to a motel. We went back out to get some dinner and got back to the motel and had some beer.

For the first time in my life I was going to make love in a hotel, with an American woman. What a thrill, I turned off the lights and opened the curtain slightly to let the light from the light pole shine through. As we were kissing and caressing, for the first time I was going to try something that was a taboo in my culture. I continued going south and gently and softly wrapped my lips around her and slowly maneuvered my tongue around her "cunani". Amelia did not realize this was the first time ever for me to do such a thing and she closed her eyes. The sight of her body undulating in front of me is still vivid in my mind. Her enjoyment of this daring and courageous act from me made me think that she might have done this before. When we were done, Amelia simply said, "That was great". I thought to myself that I was not sure if that was great because, I was afraid what was going to happen to me as a consequence of this act I just performed. In my culture, if a couple seems to be harmonious, it is said that the wife has done "Dis-oui" (Say-Yes) on the husband. In other words the husband becomes "retarded" as a result of eating a meal that contains a couple of his wife's menstrual blood drops. So the husband is said to say yes to anything the wife says, including giving his paycheck to her. I did not eat a meal containing menstrual blood drops, but I actually licked and sucked on the cunani, which I thought would cause me to be doubly "retarded". In my mind I actually went beyond the retarded. So I could not sleep, I was afraid to fall asleep for fear of becoming retarded thus saying yes to everything she would want from me.

    After trying very hard to stay awake, I eventually fell asleep. I woke up a couple of times throughout the night and went to the bathroom to look at my face in the mirror. I touched my face and turned my head side to side to view my profile to make sure nothing changed. My face was not changing to a Mongoloid skull. I made it through the night and confirmed that I definitely was not becoming retarded. In the morning I took a final look in the bathroom mirror and had a conversation with Amelia before breakfast. To test for sure nothing was going wrong with me, Amelia asked me to get her contact lenses cleaner from the backpack to her in the bathroom and I said NO and stuck with my response. She did not know why I said no and went to get the lenses cleaner herself. All throughout the day, I continued to look in the rear view mirror of the Yamaha to make sure my eye lids were not dropping or anything strange was happening to me. In all I was okay and had to re-evaluate that myth of "Dis-Oui" that I had known since I was a young boy.

    We searched for Raphael a former student of Amelia by asking every passerby if they knew of Raphael. Eventually we found someone who could take us to the compound of Raphael's family. Amelia told me Raphael and Maurice were her favorite students and wanted to see them again if they were there. Nothing appeared odd to me, as I am aware of village life and thus felt I was doing another noble deed by escorting my new American girlfriend to reconnect with a wonderful and an important part of her life. Of course part of me began to feel that tingling feeling in the guts that let one realize that you are in a competition, but I convinced myself that it was nothing and that I was the new "king of the hill" and thus had nothing to worry about! Our meeting with Raphael's family was similar to what we had experienced with the other old acquaintances of Amelia; people jumping from joy and surprise of her returning to Aplahoe. Raphael was about six feet tall, skinny, and was what one would say good-looking. Despite the obvious signs of malnutrition and the skin rash he had, Raphael could still kick my behind if it came down to it. So I played it cool, went with the flow.

    We stayed with them for about 3 hours allowing both Amelia and Raphael to touch base on past memories and the status of former students and high-school teachers. Amelia gave Raphael and his family 10,000 cfa ($20.00). We also learned that Maurice the other buddy of Raphael had quit school and was living on the coastal border between Togo and Benin where he hustled to survive. Raphael and his family were happy we stopped by and I was happy Amelia was able to locate this dear student of hers. Unfortunately to my surprise as we were getting ready to leave Raphael's family compound, somehow Amelia and Raphael suddenly left the rest of us (the rest of his family and I) as if Raphael forgot to show something to Amelia.

    My intuition led me to attempt to find them. I found them behind a hut and to my disbelief; the two were French-kissing!!! Yikes! I was shocked at what I just witnessed? I thought we were boyfriend and girlfriend, and hadn't I just performed the bravest act of my life the night before with this woman? I could have turned into a retarded man for this lady, and there she was French-kissing someone else right in my presence. I could not help but to start to cry from confusion and despair. As both of them saw me they stopped kissing and started walking back to join the rest of the people. We left that family with rather gloomy emotions as far as I was concerned.

A few minutes into our ride back to the motel, I stopped the moped in the middle of nowhere to sort out what I just experienced. I asked Amelia how she could do what she just did, and her response to me was, "what did you expect from me, I just met you two months ago, do you expect my feelings for others to just fade away?" I did not know what to do with her response except wonder what in the world I was doing in a different country with no money in my pockets and a Caucasian woman whom I started to fall in love with but who just kissed someone else few feet away from me.

We got to the motel and I remained silent for a long time. I guess Amelia realized she needed me or felt bad about her behavior and she apologized to me and asked me to forgive her. The rest of the time spent in Aplahoe was emotionless on my part, as I was afraid of being hurt again on the next visit to one of her old friends. I knew eventually that I was not going to loose her because after all we had a lot going on. She was living with me, I was her ride around the town and we still slept together.

The ride back to Lome was uneventful. The trip to the coastal border to search for Maurice, the other pal of Raphael was scheduled for the second week after our trip to Aplahoe. We took off once again early in the morning and reached Aneho around 10:00 am on a Saturday. First we had to pass by the Togolese customs office, which appeared to be stricter, as this coastal border was the main highway connecting the two countries. I showed my student ID card and Amelia showed her American passport and everything went smoothly on the Togolese side. We got on the "no-man's land" side which is a section of about 500 feet of land between the respective countries' custom offices. The place was packed with people walking in both directions crossing the border. The way it worked was all passengers must cross the no-man's-land zone on foot while both side's custom officers searched the vehicles and confirmed if need be the declared freight etc.

Once again we had neither a map nor a directions and only the name of the person we were looking for. I could not take the moped with me to the no-man's land because I did not have the proof of ownership papers with me. It was safer from the legal standpoint to park the moped on the Togolese side. If I did not do that, I may not have been able to bring the moped back into Togo as customs would have thought I bought it in Benin and was trying to bring it to Togo, or simply that it was a stolen moped thus it would have been seized. This no man's-land was the hangout of the thugs, ex-convicts and smugglers. We started to ask the ladies who sold food stuff along the road side about Maurice, and Amelia would describe him as "he is tall and dark skin with a dimple when he smiles". As I heard such a complimentary description of the unknown man who was supposed to be the classmate of Raphael who kissed my new girlfriend in front of me, the butterflies went off once again in my stomach. I convinced myself not to be paranoid.

The seventh lady we asked knew Maurice and said he rented a shack on the same compound that she did. She said she could take us there if we could wait until after she cleaned up her stall as she had sold out her rice and beans she cooked to sell to people for breakfast. So we waited for this lady to finish up. She took us to Maurice's house. We walked towards the beach through the wooded area and somehow I started feeling unsafe, as this area was the no man's-land and no law applied there. One could tell by the way people dealt with each other, the language and the survival skills of the people. We got to this area where there were about 10 shacks connected to each other. The walls were made out of woven coconut branches and the roofs were scraps corrugated iron. All of that was familiar to me because I had lived in similar conditions. Seeing people living in this type of condition did not arouse any type of emotion in me whatso ever. The walls of these shacks were such that you could see the people in the other room through the cracks between the coconut branches. If privacy was important for the occupants, they would nail flattened cardboard on the dividing wall but still one could hear anything that was happening in the other room.

We were escorted to the first shack in the set and told this was where Maurice lived. Amelia was excited and almost had tears in her eyes. Apparently Maurice was out hustling and there was no way to know exactly where he was and when he would be home. Amelia gave the lady 500 cfa ($1.00) for taking us to the house. At least now we knew where he lived, and only needed to find him in person. We walked back to the main road in no man's-land and began asking any of the hustler guys if they had seen Maurice with the assumption that they knew him. Eventually there was this big tall and dark skinned guy on the same type of Yamaha 50 as we rode to the place. He had no shirt on and was giving the ride to a woman with her baby on her back and a load of luggage on her head.

When this person saw us coming, or should I say, saw the American lady coming, he abruptly halted his moped and almost let the woman riding behind and the whole moped fall as the moped could not stop fast enough for him. Amelia screamed, "Mauriiiiice". The next thing I know they went jumping into each other's arms and became entwined in a big long hug. I was calm and collected and wore a big smile at seeing two spirits that probably meant something in each other's lives having a chance to reconnect. Amelia introduced us and we decided to go to Maurice's house. I would say Maurice was not sure at that point what was the relationship between Amelia and myself. So he was not sure whether he should hold hands with Amelia while walking or put his hands over her shoulder. Once again if it came down to it Maurice also could kick my behind. As we were getting close to Maurice's house, I could tell that he started to realize that he was taking us to a shack, a not so pleasant place to live, and he did not realize that we had been at the place before we met with him. So he started saying things as to prepare Amelia to the fact that he lived in a shack. He lived in a temporary place he said until he could save enough money to rent a "real" room somewhere. We got to the place and of course Amelia and, certainly I were not shocked about his living quarters. I sat on the only chair and Amelia and Maurice sat on the makeshift bed. Old memories were flying, and we told him that we went to Aplahoe and saw Raphael, his high school buddy. When the question came about why Maurice could not continue and finish high school, the tears started flowing. Six months after Amelia completed her Peace Corp contract and returned to the U.S., Maurice lost his mother, the only support he had and he did not have anyone to support him through school. As hard as I tried to hold my tears, after hearing his story, I could not help it and the three of us started crying. Of course I could not allow myself to cry as loudly as both of them so I only allowed my tears to flow without restraint. I could say that was a uniting moment.

Even though I had just met Maurice, I could sympathize with him, as I understood what he had gone through since I had been through enough hardship that made me understand his situation. After the tears, we decided to go get some food and have some beer before we headed back to Lome. We walked back toward the main road, bought food from the women who vend food, and ate by the side of the road. We ate Coun, corn meal dish with fried fish and tomato sauce and three bottles of beer. Typically, Amelia and I would share a large bottle of beer. On this occasion she had her own bottle. Amelia paid for the food and gave Maurice about $20.00 worth of cfa.

We decided it was time to return to the Togolese side of the border and pickup the moped before it got too dark. As the three of us were walking west toward the Togolese border, Maurice saw some of his friends inside a bar. They called his name and yelled out that they wanted to exchange a couple of words. He wanted to go show his friends his ex-high school teacher so he hurriedly pulled Amelia to go introduce her to those guys and quickly returned so we would not be late getting back to the Togolese side. I kind of stood behind and watched them went. As I was waiting for them to come back to no avail, I decided to go see what was going on; maybe they got caught up in a long conversation. Surprise, surprise the two were French kissing. It was almost as if Maurice forced the kissing issue but the fact was that they were still kissing till I got in the bar! What should I do now? I was very embarrassed, shocked, sadden, and disgusted. I knew I could not make an ass of myself by displaying my anger as the Maurice guy could beat me up easily and I had more to loose. I remembered when Amelia mentioned to me in Aplahoe "she just met me and what I was expecting."

The ride back to Lome was quite silent. My reality was that I did not really have experience with the dating scene and did not know what to really expect. One thing I was sure of was that this lady did me wrong and I was convinced that the poor man should not expect much. So I "sucked" it up and managed to start talking to this woman. The fact was that she was living with me; I do not know how to kick anyone out. After all being with her had improved my English and my status amongst my peers. I was the guy who was dating the American girl. The image of my father throwing my mother's belongings out of the house onto the street was on my mind and I did not want to be like my father. I will never treat a woman like my mother was treated on that incident. Somehow I viewed this opportunity with Amelia as a test of that conviction of mine to see if I would behave just like my father. I did not behave just like my father; I kept my cool, and went with the flow.

After all, being with Amelia improved my self-esteem somewhat as I never would think any woman would want to date me since I did not have a decent place or money to take care of a woman. Amelia had two more weeks in Lomé before returning to the U.S. Amelia apologized for a second time for her not so tactful kissing behavior and I accepted her apology and life went on. Amelia realized that any other man would have persisted with the drama and made her time in Togo hellish. But because, I did not behave like she expected, she started to really like me. Amelia thought I was special, that I was different and as her time in Lome was getting shorter and shorter, she started to fall in love with me she said. Amelia left for the U.S. and we promised to stay in touch. She said she was going to finish her Master's degree at UCLA and return to Togo to stay with me until I finished college then we would both go to the U.S. where we would live. I was in love with Amelia because I believed she liked me because of who I was not because of what I had since I did not have anything. I wrote her a letter every week, to let her know how my life was going.

I resumed classes at the University and I was more confident in myself because I could understand English. I was in tune with what was going on in the rest of the world by continuing watching ABC news every Friday and I had a girlfriend in America who promised to come back to me. Financially when Amelia left, my situation was back to what it was before. I had to juggle between the small amounts of money my mother and sisters gave me and the pure generosity of people. I believe I was a humble person and others appreciated that quality in me and would share food with me when I did not have any. One thing I was sure of was that when it became financially tough for me, I knew I could always go to see my mother and sisters at the market of Bè and they would get me something to eat and give me some pocket money.

I became the romantic guy and a serious guy at the same time. I did not allow any situation that could give any woman I got in contact with a false impression that I was interested in her, as I did not want anything to come between Amelia and me. I promised myself that I would never duplicate the polygamist lifestyle my father led.

I attributed the fact that my two younger sisters and I did not get the attention we needed because my father wanted another son and left my mother for another woman. He needed another son so that just in case I died, there would be another one of his children to carry on the family name. I stayed focused, but at times it got more difficult as there were some beautiful college students around. But that stress faded away quickly as I realized that I was broke and could not afford to date anyone anyway. One needed to at least be able to buy the woman a glass of ice water on a hot day, and believe it or not I could not afford even that on a consistent basis. I came to accept wet dreams as an acceptable phenomenon for someone in my situation. Amelia sent me music tapes of Smokey Robinson, Steve Wonder, George Benson and Chorus Line. These tapes helped me a lot emotionally as they had love songs that comforted me and helped me deal with the distance between Amelia and me. I played these tapes over and over to the point that I could whistle every note of George Benson's guitar on his album. I could sing along to all the songs on the Chorus Line's album.

On campus I tried to ask every student that I met if they had a telephone in their house or if they knew of anyone in the government that does not pay for their telephone. It turned out that my roommate's stepbrother, who brought him to Lomé to attend College, was the Assistant Secretary of Energy of Togo. My roommate Itab took me to his stepbrother's house where he would arrange for me to make a phone call to Amelia in Los Angeles. Simply writing letters to Amelia was not enough; I needed to hear her voice and I had to find other people like Itab to setup telephone call opportunities. The best opportunity was when my former high school pal introduced me to the telephone operator at the Presidential Palace. At first I thought this guy was a fake, as one would not have thought anyone who works at the Presidential palace would appear so poor and in fact be so poor. The guy would ask me to "do something" and I would hustle to scrounge up at times 200 cfa ($.60) or at times 500 cfa (about $1.00) to give him. What we did was I would have to find someone who had a telephone in their house and give him their telephone number. He would call Amelia in Los Angeles and then call me and connect our phones. Then I could talk to Amelia for hours. It was scary as hell as I knew I could have been thrown into jail for such an act, and deservedly so. (I would not recommend doing this to anyone, it was wrong).

I can definitely say that I am here now and writing by the grace of God and I will tell you why.

One Tuesday Morning, in September 1987, around 10:00 AM, I left my apartment for the main post office to mail a letter to Amelia. I was riding my moped going down the hill leading to the downtown area. As soon as I went over the bridge that separated the downtown area from the "hill-top" section of the city, I noticed a huge crowd screaming, "We've got him! We've got him!" Subsequently I parked my moped to investigate what was going on, as the main road was pretty much swamped with people and I could not have passed anyway. I asked a woman who was selling Colico (fried yams) alongside the street what was going on.

A military truck passed by and I thought it was just going into the army camp. The army camp entrance was about 200 feet on the left side of the main road going south. All of a sudden, the soldiers in the back of the military truck started to shoot in the air to disperse the crowd. That was the first time I heard gunshots in real life. The crowd started to run north, and so I took off facing north where I was coming from. Then the shooting increased, and we all realized very quickly that we would not be able to make it pass the bridge. There were shots coming from everywhere now and no one could tell where the shots were coming from. So instead of continuing north on the bridge and risk to be killed, I jumped off the road followed by a bunch of other people in panic. I could not go far onto the grassy swamp alongside the lagoon. The swamp area was where unfortunately many people from the nearby marketplace went to make a bowel movement. There were human feces all over the place but that did not matter at all at that point. I dove onto the ground and wished that I had some magical power that would make me sink into the ground.

The shooting intensified and sounded like machine guns going tatata tatata tatata, followed by the air-piercing sounds of the bullets. There was a tree at about 10 feet away from me and I could see the bullets piercing the trunk of the tree at a height of three to four feet from the ground. I could not even cry as everything was going so fast, so I thought of my mother who did not know where I was, and I wondered if Amelia would ever know that I got killed on my way to mail a letter to her! I made my last prayer to God, as I was sure I was going to die. I asked forgiveness for all the sins I might have committed and prayed that God would watch over my mother, sisters, and Amelia.

The letter to Amelia was still on the back of my moped on the other side of the street and I was about 600 feet from the moped. No one would know that the moped belonged to me except that I had the ignition key in my pocket. I did not even have the chance to lock the moped prior to the shooting beginning. I remained still on top of feces on the moist ground next to the lagoon as the shooting went on for about 30 minutes or so. All of a sudden it got quiet. I realized I was not dead. I lifted my head to look toward the main road and saw the crowd running to cross the bridge.

Women were dragging their children who could not keep up with the running speed. Everyone was running for his or her lives, going northward. People were going to toward the north side of the lagoon because there was a house there and people could seek refuge in the houses. On the south side of the lagoon, were the Marketplace, the big movie theater and the military camp. So it made sense that people who needed refuge would run to the other side of the lagoon where the houses were located.

The key to survival for me at that point was to join the crowd and run with everybody to the other side of the lagoon. So I got off the ground and sprinted as fast as I could to join the running crowd. I have never ran as fast like that in my entire life. We were all running leaning forward as if by doing so we would minimize our chances of being hit by bullets. Just as we were about to reach the north bank of the lagoon the shooting resumed. There was a sewage system around the lagoon and in normal conditions; it would have been impossible for anyone like me to simply jump over this seven-foot open sewer. I did jump over this sewer as if it was nothing at all and followed the crowd into the first house.

Everyone was just trying to find a place to hide to avoid being killed. I was wearing the Batakaly sleeveless Kente strip shirt that Amelia gave me and a pair of used jeans that I bought a while ago. I managed to get into a room in the compound of this house. As I dropped to the ground to get under the bed in the room, I realized that someone else was there already. He tried to push me away as if doing so would have made him safer.

I told him in a quiet imperative voice that he needed to stop pushing me, as we all were trying to find a safe place to be. So he did not push me any more. We both laid there under the bed quietly and we could hear people's hearts beating loudly between the rounds of shooting.

I still was not sure what the hell was going on. I thought of mercenaries invading the country in an attempt to overthrow the government. About a half-hour later, we heard the siren of an ambulance and then someone yelled that it was over and to come out. I heard a bunch of people talking outside and was convinced that it was ok to come out from the under the bed. As I came out of this room, in my "American Peace Corp volunteer wanna be" outfit (most Peace Corp volunteers wore Batakaly), a man pointed at me and said, "That one looks like one of them." In that split second I had to convince everyone that I was not one of anything or I would have been beaten to death. Luckily I had my student ID with me and I started speaking Mina, my native language, to them. I told them the name of my father's village and that my mother and sisters were merchants in the market of Bè. I told them that I was simply on my way to the main post office and in fact my moped was still along side of the road on the other side of the lagoon. I had to say all that very fast to convince them.

Just as I finished quickly conveying my story to them and adding that I was a victim just as they were, the shooting resumed and once again everyone had to run for shelter. This time the previous room I hid in was not close enough and I follow the crowd to this small corner between houses, and found what appeared to have been a converted old bathroom where benches were kept. This tiny little storage room was packed with people, all quiet and terrified. Everyone was trying to get to the back of this tiny room. I figured if I could manage to put my head under the benches that, any bullet would have to come through a whole bunch of people first before it hits my head. I got on the floor and despite the kicking; I twisted my body to get my head and chest area under the benches. The shooting intensified and we could hear the sound of bullets bouncing against the corrugated iron roofs in the compound.

A while later the other person who managed to get himself under the benches along with me called out, "Would the person who is urinating on me please quit urinating on me?" It turned out that it was no urine. One of the people at the top of the pile said, "I think I am hit", and he continued to bleed heavily. We had heard the siren of the ambulance earlier, and we realized that the only way this man could survive was to get him out of the hiding place to the open where hopefully they could get him to the ambulance. I could not see his face but this situation took over all of our fear. Suddenly the group of people that did not even know each other agreed by silent consensus that this gentleman should get out to get help for himself. We advised him that he had a better chance of surviving by going out than staying with us.

This was the real moment of truth for all of us, as we cared enough for him that we thought he should get out, yet we all knew that by going out, there was a chance that he might die sooner than if he stayed with us. The consensus prevailed to convince him he better get out and seek help. He got the courage to limp out of the tiny hiding place. I prayed for him.

After about forty long minutes, we again heard someone calling out for people to get out and go home. We were hesitant but eventually people started slowly to get out. I did not want to be the last one getting out of there so I got up and began walking and realized that my shirt and pants were soaked in blood. That did not stop me. Once again we all ran to the outside of this compound. The Togolese soldier in a camouflage outfit was directing people to go north and go home. So I took off running like everyone else. I ran non-stop all the way to my place. As I passed by people who were standing in front of their homes wondering what was going on, they saw me covered with blood, and thought I was hurt. I just kept running till I got home. I would say I ran for about 5 miles non-stop. When I reached my neighborhood, and people saw me covered with blood, they followed me to my apartment compound to find out what was going on. My landlady had a bar connected to the house. I sat down in the bar and as I was explaining the hellish experience I just went through, an older man in my audience asked me to tell him exactly where my moped was parked. He offered to go and bring my moped back to me. I kind of laughed at him inside my head. The man was about 65 years old and a retired soldier who I thought should not dare be going to the "war zone" I had just come from. He said it was no problem that I should stay put and he would get my moped back to me. A 65-year-old man in Africa is very old.

Before the old man departed the old man took my key and his last shot of liquor as he took off on foot. I went and took a shower and changed my clothes. I was still in shock from the near death experience and could not believe how I survived all that. Three hours later, indeed the retired soldier came back with my moped. I started to cry, I did not know what to say to him. I was so proud of him and wondered how he managed to go through that area to get to the moped that I had left unlocked. He laughed and responded that he was a military man and that he could go anywhere he needed to go! I did not have a lot of money but I could afford to buy him a large bottle of beer in gratitude.

The letter I was going to mail to Amelia was still inside the book on the back seat of the moped. As I picked up the book with the letter, I thought to myself that I almost died all for love. If I had not gone to mail the letter, I would not have gone through the crazy episode I just described. On the evening news it was reported that there were mercenaries who came from the neighboring country of Ghana to overthrow the government. They were out-maneuvered by the Togolese armed forces. About 19 people were killed including a woman who was found dead on the ground with her infant baby alive and feeding at her breast. How did I survive all that? I am still wondering and am grateful.

For the next couple of days, I could not leave the house. I was scared to death. The government reported that the bad guys were arrested and a couple of them were shown on the nightly news on television. School continued for me and I continued communicating with Amelia via telephone and letters.

Amelia finally finished her Masters program at UCLA and was ready to get a job. She returned to the East Coast of the United States where her parents lived. She got a job offer in

Washington, D.C. with the World Health Organization but she turned it down. She revealed to me that the reason she turned down the job offer was that she was afraid if she accepted the job she would have to have me come to the U.S.

Amelia told me she could not accept this because, as a Peace Corp volunteer all the men she met, wanted to marry her so they could come to the U.S. In a way that was true because, as I said earlier, we all grew up hoping to finish high school and somehow go to France and then come back to Togo where we would get office jobs. Associating with a Caucasian person meant that one had the chance to escape the poverty and hopelessness that was so prevalent. She told me that instead of taking the job in Washington, she wanted to come to Togo to stay with me until I finished college. Then hopefully we both could come to the U.S.

eibBooks.com

As in Electronic Instant Books
As in eXcellence In Book Selling

Get your book published online instantly, electronically and/or in paperback format like this book and sell it directly on Zongo*Me*.com

We show you how!

CHAPTER FIVE

      Finally Amelia indeed came back to Togo and now we had to find a better place to live. We drove around the city on my moped and found an apartment that Amelia was interested in. We would pay 45,000 cfa (about $85.00)/month for the villa. Somehow Amelia had saved money while going to school. I was not sure what it meant for someone to have a job and still go to school. I did not have that opportunity. We moved into our new villa and all of a sudden it was like we were married. We were living like married couple in the Togolese tradition. On a trip to Cotonou, the Capital City of the Republic of Benin, to go see my father who was living there in financial exile, Amelia and I bought us a pair of gold wedding rings. She said they were a show of our love for each other. When my father saw the rings he asked us if we were married. We said that we were not and that the rings were just symbols of our love for each other. I really had no clue what marriage meant at that time, as I had no model to refer to.

      You see, my father did not have the opportunity to pursue his education beyond third grade. His father died when he was young and his mother could not pay the school fees for him to continue school. So he went farming with his mother to survive. When he was a teenager, he was sent to become an apprentice bricklayer. I only knew my father as the bricklayer. Somehow my father had this idea he called "tontine" which means little savings. My father would go around on his bicycle to the marketplaces and collect money from the women vending in the market every day. Each woman at the marketplace decided how much money she wanted to put aside everyday. It could be $.50 or $.75 or $1.00. The first "little savings" deposit my father collected became his commission and at the end of the month he would return the balance of the total amount he collected to each person. Since the average person did not have the required skills to deal with the official banking system this tontine concept seemed to satisfy a need for the uneducated women merchants of the marketplaces around the city. The tontine was based on

The Way It Was *Coming To America:* The Real Story.

TRUST between my father and his customers. The women trusted him and he became so popular that he had a lot of customers. My father began for the first time to do well. When I saw my father doing his tontine job he had a big black bag over his shoulder similar to the mailman and he was on his bicycle. My father would collect all the people's money every day and mark down on a notebook each customer's contribution. When he got to his house, would count the money and put the money in a bucket and hide it inside his bedroom.

Apparently my father's stepson, who was a teenager and delinquent, came back to my father's house and figured out where my father was hiding the money. He stole the bucket of other people's money from my father. Well, there was not a legal system to which his customers could turn to; so if they saw him, they would start beating him up and possibly kill him for stealing their money. In this form of justice, the criminal is beaten and continues to be beaten during the escort to the police station. So my father had to flee to the Republic of Benin together with his wife and five children. The oldest stepson disappeared and no one could find him.

It was in the second year of my father's exile to Benin that Amelia and I went to visit him. I felt it was important for my father to see that I had a girlfriend who actually returned from the U.S. to be with me. When we got back from the visit to my father, my sisters and mother noticed the wedding rings and asked if we got married without informing them. We told them that we were not married. Amelia and I decided to inquire about civil marriage at the city hall. We went and got the necessary papers and got home and never followed through. . I had no idea what I was supposed to do and Amelia was hesitant because of her past experiences with African men. Besides coming back to Togo to be with me, Amelia also had the need to complete a field study in order to fully complete her Masters degree from UCLA. The topic of her research paper was "Childhood diarrhea and its treatment among the Ewe people of Togo". She was to pick two villages to conduct the research. The only place we thought we would start was Notse the city village where we were with the

The Way It Was *Coming To America:* The Real Story.

UCLA Educational Abroad Program students. We had to wait until the summer so that school was over for me before we could venture to the countryside. When we got to Notse, I realize that it was probably a good idea to go to the mayor's office to inform him of what we were going to be doing in the villages. I explained that Amelia's research would enable her to have a better understanding of diarrhea and that the way it was treated would give insight for her to present to her professors at UCLA. The mayor was honored that we took the initiative to come and contact him first before we started our project. He gave us his blessing. We told him that we were going to focus on the villages of Dalia and Tchiniga. Dalia is about 25 miles southeast of Notse and Tchiniga is about 75 miles West of Notse. The two villages were selected from a drawing out of a hat.

    When we got to Dalia the closest village to Notse, we went to the village chief to introduce ourselves and inform him of the purpose of our visit. There had never been a Caucasian who visited Dalia. We asked permission to talk to the women and we also needed to convey to the chief that we were not affiliated with the government to minimize the fear of potential taxation or anything of that sort. Amelia brought with her a recording Walkman and a lot of blank tapes. We counted all the huts in the village and drew a map of the village. Amelia was determined to make sure that the women we talked to were selected randomly and to me it did not make any difference at that point. We were to talk to women who were actually mothers with young children. Amelia would ask questions and I would translate them into Ewe for the women. I spoke Ewe to the women and would translate their responses into English for Amelia. The basic interview would start with a greeting and my brief description of the reason why Amelia was there, not me but Amelia, for the people could care less about the average Joe I was. I would ask, "How would you describe your child's diarrhea." The women would just fall out as they were laughing and say things like "the Yovos are indeed silly. Why would anyone travel all the way from America to come ask a question about diarrhea?" With a calm face controlling my urge to laugh also, I would convey via a calm and serious voice tone that, the interviews were for Amelia's education purpose and the result of the research might help the Americans have a better understanding of diarrhea. I emphasized that she would have learned all this information from them. We always asked the interviewee the permission to tape the interview and they were happy to let us do so. We did not spend the nights in Dalia, we returned at the end of the day to Notse where we made arrangements to stay at the under-utilized teacher training facility which was cheaper than staying in a motel.

In Dalia we met Papa Koffi who was a retired army veteran that supposedly had fought for the French in the Algerian war. Papa Koffi could speak broken French and took it upon himself to follow us to every interview, as he needed to make sure that we were not coming to either contaminate the mind of the women or ask questions that were not part of our intended interview questions. The village nurse was considered a Physician and was given a lot of respect. As we came to the section of the village on the last portion of our chart, we found a relatively young man naked, muddy and chained at the waist to the trunk of a tree. We asked Papa Koffi, why was he chained and the response was that he was a crazy person and the only way to keep him safe was to keep him chained to the tree.

We asked why he wasn't wearing any clothes; he said anytime his mother dressed him he would take off the clothes and tear them up. When it rains then someone would unchain him from the tree and take him inside a small mud hut where he would be chained to a pole. When the crazy man saw Amelia, he started to sing and dance and started to speak French. His French was better than Papa Koffi's French. He would say things like "Hello, My name is John, I am the captain of this airplane, please fasten your seatbelt." Apparently, he managed to finish high school in Notse and went to the capital city and was recruited to join the army. He had wanted to become a fighter-jet pilot but somehow, as Papa Koffi reported to us, jealousy in the Village had caused a witch to put a spell on him and that caused him to become crazy and he missed the opportunity to become a fighter pilot. The interview in Dalia went pretty well and the women very nicely received us. We collected valuable data, mostly tape-recorded. In all we spent a whole week in Dalia. The next phase of our countryside trip was to head for Tchiniga. We knew Tchiniga was going to be a real adventure. The only thing we knew of the place was that it was about 75 miles west of Notse. We simply asked people at the marketplace in Notse how to get to Tchiniga and were told to simply follow the road going west and we would get there. We filled up the gas tank of the moped got some fruit and water and we packed the backpack with some clothes. We did not have a spare tire or a spare container of gasoline, which today I would say was a very crazy thing to do.

    We were venturing at this point into the unknown. If we had a flat tire on the way, there was no way we could get back to Notse to get it fixed as the pickup trucks that ran that route to transport people only does it once a week. We hit the road around 9:00 am with the hope that we would get there before dark. I had to give it to Amelia, as she was a real trooper. I would say her training at Peace Corp has prepared her well for all of the adventures we have been on. She ate anything I ate i.e. any Togolese dish, and was ready for the challenge. Somehow I had faith in God that nothing would happen to the moped and nothing did. That moped was "my friend". I knew how to handle that moped and we understood each other. I did not abuse the moped; I used theories of physics to handle my moped on the road.

    To make sure we did not miss Tchiniga, we would ask the few farmers we passed by if we were on the right track. They would say that we were and we kept going. The road was bumpy and at times nothing but grass and I tried not to ride on any thorny grass that would cause me a flat tire. We were so deep far into our trip that any flat tire would have meant spending the night standing in the middle of the woods. We eventually arrived at Tchiniga around 3:30 p.m. As people saw us, they went to the "Yovo, Yovo bonsoir ca va bien merci" song. Amelia hated that song and even I hated that song We asked to be taken to the chief of the village so we could talk to him and make arrangements for a place to spend the night. We did not know these people, yet we were confident that we would be provided a place to stay.

Remember I mentioned earlier that my Togolese culture believes that one should treat a traveler with a kind heart because one never knows when he or she would be a traveler in someone else's area. In general the chief in a village is the oldest or one of the elder members of the village.

When we went to this chief's house, I could not tell if he was very old as he had dyed his hair black like mothers do to their children on Christmas Eve. Mothers would take their children to the market to have their hair dyed black to hide any signs of malnutrition so the children look healthy. My mother use to have my hair dyed and the lady who dyed hair (the Yombo lady) made sure she gave the boys a nice fat dyed sideburn. Sometimes she made them as fat as Elvis Presley's sideburns so kids would have dyed sideburns for a couple of days until it faded out.

As we were introduced to the chief, and started talking, Amelia gave him a compliment that he looked quite young for a chief. He then told us that he was 65 years old. As was customary when you have a guest, the guest is offered water to quench their thirst from a long journey. There was a young lady who brought us the water. We noticed when we first got to the chief's compound, two of the chief's wives came to greet us and stayed for a while and went back to what they were doing. Then there was this young lady who brought us the water.

Amelia and I had this trick that we played to avoid getting sick when we were offered water from the villagers. We would pretend that we were drinking the water by merely touching our lips to the cup and swallowing our saliva while doing so; then I made sure when I poured the water onto the ground for the ancestors, I poured enough so the host could not determine how much water we did not drink. We had our own bottled water that we packed and that we rationed to last the entire stay. As the conversation went on, we asked if the young lady and the young man Noel were the chief's children. The chief laughed and informed us that the young man Noel was indeed his 18-year-old youngest child and the 17-year-old young lady was his youngest wife. Amelia was smiling while she asked the question to the chief. I could see her smile freeze upon hearing the response and then her face turned red. Even I could not believe what I just heard being that I am a Togolese guy. We left that alone and proceed to explain to the chief the reason why we were there and that we obviously would need a place to stay overnight.

The chief assured us that lodging was not an issue and that we were welcome to be his guest. We gave the chief four loaves of bread, two bottles of whisky and a bag of smoked fish that we bought at the market in Notse. Simple gestures like that go along way. The chief gave orders to his son Noel to prepare the mud hut to the westward edge of the village for us. We took our stuff into the room and were amazed by the hospitality of these people.

At about 6:30 p.m., the chief's first wife brought us dinner, which comprised of Akumey and Yebessessi (polenta with ground up tomato and pepper with grilled dry fish). We ate dinner and were grateful. While Noel was helping us setup our room, we asked him with sarcasm if the 17 year old girl was his stepmother, and he said that his father had helped heal a man from another village with some herbal medicine and the man was so grateful that he gave his daughter to the chief in marriage as a sign of his appreciation. Around 7:30 p.m., Noel came to tell us that we were invited to sit in the traditional healing session of a neighbor's child who had been sick and did not seem to be getting better. As we stepped out of our room, we saw that Noel was teaching some children how to read. We also heard that Noel was the village's teacher because he was the only one that could read. Noel was sent to Notse to go to school and could only complete fourth grade because his father, the chief, could not afford to support him in Notse.

He returned to his village to stay with his parents. Noel was vibrant, full of energy and had a big smile. He was one of those people you could see had great potential but did not have the proper support. Noel with his fourth grade education was considered the teacher of the village and he took pride in teaching the children how to read and how to count. It was a moving experience to see that. So we walked in the dark with our flashlight to the neighbor's house where the village Voodoo man was going to conduct the healing session for the sick girl. The girl must have been about 7 – 8 years old and was lying on her mother's lap looking very miserable. They had just started the session before we entered the hut. A lantern lit the room and Noel directed us to sit on the stool in the corner as spectators. The Voodoo man was wearing a raffia skirt and had decorated his face with white chalk. He held a small white horse tale switch in his left hand and a grass straw broom in the other hand. He was singing as we entered the room. He sang and circled the mother and child, sang some more and circled them some more. He then burned some herbs, which I now know were sage and other herbs. Amelia leaned over to tell me that this child looked dehydrated.

Throughout our journey, Amelia taught me the best thing to do was to give the child a lot of fluids and if possible add a little salt and sugar to the water to treat a case of dehydration caused by severe diarrhea. In fact we had in our backpack a couple of packs of hydrating fluid specifically for cases of severe diarrhea. So we sat there and watched the Voodoo man do his thing, we asked Noel quietly how long had the child been sick, and he said about four days.

The Voodoo man left the room and returned with some leaves of Kpatima which was the common leaf used to cleanse the spirit. One simply put Kpatima leaves in cold water and washed oneself or poured the water on the head or simply washed the hands. The Voodoo man dipped the leaves into a pot full of water and shook the wet leaves over the mother and child as if startling the child with the cold water would cause the child to be more alert. Nothing happened; he sang some more and went around the mother and child some more, nothing happened. Now he decided he needed to do some reading of Afa, which is the tossing of cowry shells with a spell to communicate with the spiritual world. Depending on the number of shells that landed on their backs, he could determine what the Afa spirit wanted. So he asked the Afa if this child' sickness was a natural disease or a human caused sickness i.e. was it caused by witchcraft. His reading revealed it was caused by witchcraft. Next, he needed to find out what he could offer to the witch in exchange for the child's spirit. After another tossing of the cowry shells, the Voodoo man announced that the witch would accept the sacrifice of a rooster at a crossroads; a bottle of Sodabee and that, the child's father had to be cleansed with the Kpatima water. He said that after the offering at the crossroad no one should look back on the way back to the house. The Voodoo man took a sip of Sodabee and sprayed it out of his mouth onto the ground as if spraying the alcohol into the eyes of the bad spirits would chase them away. Sodabbee is a distilled palm wine, similar to Vodka I would say. It is said that when the first British tasted this ever so popular liquor he exclaimed "oh, so that be!" and the locals thought he meant the liquor's name was SODABBEE and until today, that liquor is called Sodabbee.

Amelia and I stayed put; she whispered to me that the child probably needed some fluid in her system. We could not say or do anything as we were invited as observers and that was how the "system" had worked for generations. Noel was sent to fetch a rooster and when he got back, the men left the house through the darkness singing on their way to the crossroads; the child was laid on a mat. When they came back about 30 minutes later, the child was still motionless. The Voodoo man sang more songs. We got tired and had to leave to go to bed. We went to our room, brushed our teeth with bottled water and went to bed. The mattress was made out of a burlap bag filled with dried grass straw. We had packed with us a pot to urinate in during the night, which we emptied out in the morning. But this time Amelia needed to make number two in the middle of the night.

Well, when we were first taken to our guestroom, Noel had shown us the place where to use bathroom. It was just in the woods about forty feet behind our hut. They had pigs out there that ate up the bowels once the person was done. The problem was that there was competition between the pigs and each pig wants to get the poop first which causes the pooper to have a stick to chase away the pigs while they are taking care of business. Since I did not plan this middle of the night session, I had no stick to chase the pigs away. I had a flashlight that I shone on Amelia who was sitting in a squatted position taking care of business. She was scared to death and I had to keep the pigs away from her. It was so dark outside, and the only noises were from the owls and the grunting of the pigs. I started to feel scared but convinced myself, that I could not be scared; I had to be the man. So I did my manly duty and kept the pigs away, and we finally got back to the house and slept for the rest of the night.

    The next morning Noel was waiting for us to wake up and sadly informed us that the girl had died. We both felt very bad, we knew that if we had suggested that child should be forced to take in some fluids that could have saved her life but that it was not our place to do so, and we sat helplessly through that whole experience the night before. Besides we were only going to be there for a few days. We were not visiting as nurses or doctors, merely as a research student and her assistant/translator.

    We thought that even if the men would have given us the opportunity to take care of the child, first of all it would not have been me because, I was just one of them, and secondly, it would have been Amelia, a woman, who would have "taken over" the village Voodoo Man's place". After we are gone, the village would have been in worse shape because the credibility of the Voodoo man would be perceived as undermined, and the village would have nothing to fall back on as far as health care was concerned. We took this girl's death very personally although we thought she would have died any way even if we did not show up in the village that same night! May she rest in peace!

    Our interviews with the women in this village were nothing like the ones we had in Dalia. We realized that Tchiniga was smaller than Dalia. The interviews there were not as interesting as what we were used to. We persevered and did about 45 interviews. One thing we noticed also was that we needed to wake up earlier than we did because the women left very early in the morning to go to their farms. At the end of our interviews the same day it became necessary that we leave Tchiniga to go back to Notse. We went around thanking all those we needed to thank, and hit the road. Noel was depressed to see us leave as we brought excitement to his life. He was the only one in the village that could communicate directly with Amelia in French. The moped ride back to Notse was less stressful this time, as we knew where we were going. We spent one night in Notse and headed for Lomé the following day. When we got back to Lomé Amelia applied for a teaching position at the American cultural center to teach English as second language.

We continued to live together in Lomé, where I went to the university for classes and Amelia went downtown to teach English at the American cultural center.

eibBooks.com
As in Electronic Instant Books
As in eXcellence In Book Selling

Get your book published online instantly, electronically and/or in paperback format like this book and sell it directly on Zongo*Me*.com

We show you how!

PART TWO

On My Way to America

CHAPTER SIX

*O*n the campus I heard of an International Camp Counselors Program which was a program sponsored by YMCA America to bring summer camp counselors from around the world into the U.S. to work in summer camps as exchange students. The English Department of my University and the American Cultural Center coordinated this program. The English Department students would take an English proficiency test at the Cultural Center and those who scored passing scores would get to come to the U.S. for the summer. The students would work at the summer camps, have free room and board, and were paid $250.00 at the end of the program. As a joke, I wanted to take that proficiency test even though I was a history major and had just started taking some courses at the English Department. They told me I could if I wanted to. So I did and I scored the second highest on the proficiency test and was informed that I would be going to the U.S. that summer as a camp counselor. Wow, I said, did that mean I would be on an airplane, me, child of my mother? I was amazed! I could not believe this news.

The cultural center staff told me that I would need to submit my picture and fill out some resume forms that would be sent out to summer camp directors in the U.S. If a camp director selected us, then they would send us an affidavit of support that we would use to request a tourist visa from the U.S. embassy. When I got home I informed Amelia that I got accepted to go to the U.S. for the summer as a camp counselor. I thought Amelia would have been happy for me but she was not. She thought I was joking, and I said, no this was a lifetime opportunity for me and that I would be going. She asked what was going to happen to her. I told her to stay in Togo and wait for me.

She freaked out and could not believe that I could even conceive of leaving her in Togo by herself while I was in the U.S. In my African mind then, I felt this woman ought to be out of her mind to think that a poor man like myself would throw away an opportunity like that for whatever reason! I was determined to come to America. I reminded Amelia, as my attempt to make a point, that she had the chance to see me in my environment; I believed that going to the U.S. for the summer would enable me to better learn about her culture and thus understand her better! I made all the necessary preparations for my trip.

    Somehow Amelia still was not convinced that I was actually going to go to the U.S. with the ICCP program. My family was still in disbelief about their child flying on an airplane to go to America. I got my ticket and affidavit of support from YMCA, got my visa for 90 days in the U.S. My mother was proud but I could tell that she was worried that her only son was going to travel that far, so she gave me four Shakere gourds and some glass bead bracelets she made with the thought that I could sell them in America if I needed some money for food.

    The night before I left for the US, Amelia and I made love without using a condom because we were out of them and we were also out of spermicidal cream she used with the diaphragm. It was the last time that we made love since I would be gone for 90 days.

    We took the taxi to the airport and my mother and four sisters met us there. I was nervous first for leaving Amelia, and second for having to go on an airplane. Around 11:30PM the announcement was made for people to start boarding the airplane. I said goodbye to my people and boarded the airplane. As we took off a thunderstorm started. My stomach felt like there was a giant hole in it as the plane took off. Suddenly, I saw lighting and the plane kind of shook as if we just lost altitude. I was sitting in the middle isle and had people on both sides of me. On my left was a Nigerian businessman who was returning to London and on my right was a lady returning to France. The "hole" in my stomach felt like it got deeper as we were gaining more altitude. I sat up straight in my seat to make sure the plane was not going down or anything while I was just sitting there passively not attempting to save myself. Both people next to me were so calm and I was so scared and thought we were for sure falling from the sky. I could not hide my fear any longer so I asked the guy to my left why was he so calm, and why wasn't he concerned about the jerkiness of the airplane. He replied to me that he traveled all the time and was used to that kind of thing. Then I thought, I guess it was normal for airplanes to shake due to turbulence. I managed to calm myself.

Eventually the flight attendant came around and asked us for our beverage of choice. The gentleman on my left side requested champagne. I thought he was being ridiculous for wanting champagne. I asked for just plain water, as I was not going to be sucked into buying an expensive drink. I only had $3.00 worth of money on me for my 90-day trip to America. I chose not to ask Amelia for any pocket money for the trip as she had to pay the rent and due to the fact that she was not happy about me coming to America. I figured she probably would not have given me money anyway.

We landed at JFK international Airport and I was greeted by YMCA staff and driven to the YMCA hotel on Sloan Avenue in New York City. I was given a room where I was to stay until I took the bus the following day to Springfield Massachusetts. After I got into my room at the YMCA, I noticed there was a TV in there and felt extra special. TV's were a luxury in Togo, as many people simply did not have them. I took the used camera I bought before the trip and left the YMCA hotel to explore the city streets. I got downstairs and was amazed at how crowded New York City was and how fast the cars were running.

I started taking pictures of the tall buildings that I thought I needed to take to convince people back in Togo when I returned that I was actually in New York City. As I walked down 42nd street, I noticed that the streets were getting more crowded, and I got a bit nervous because the last time I saw a crowd like that in Togo I almost died. So, I quickly convinced myself that I was in America and nothing like that could happen here. I walked cautiously towards the crowd and discovered that the crowd was watching a parade. The police blocked the streets to protect the parade. I saw people on tops of trailer truck beds dressed up in leather and feather outfits with a lot of make up on their faces, men and women alike. I asked the people around me what the parade was for, and was told it was the International Parade of Gays and Lesbians. I asked what did Gay and Lesbian mean, and the people looked at me up and down, as if I had just asked the ridiculous question in the world. I knew the word "gaie" in French meant someone who was happy and that was the most I knew of that sound at that time.

Lesbian, I had no clue what that meant, so I persisted with my questioning to other people and eventually an older lady who had the courage to tell me that Gays and Lesbians meant homosexuals. Then I was confused, I wondered why would people be telling the world that they were homosexual, wasn't that kind of embarrassing and to see that these people were dancing on top of trucks with signs clearly telling the spectators things like "Gay & Lesbian Lawyers from London", "Gay & Lesbian Police Officers", was disturbing. Then I noticed that on-duty police officers were protecting the parade. It dawned to me that the police were actually protecting the Gay & Lesbian parade. Then, it sank into my whole being that yes, indeed I was in America, the land of the free. This was the place where everyone was free to express themselves, without fear of being stoned to death or thrown into jail without any legal representation. For a moment the thought of real freedom scared me and the excitement of being in America for the first time in my life felt like it was put temporarily on hold. I was walking back to the hotel and saw a black limousine go by and no one stood still on the side of the road while it went by. I asked a passerby if that was the president in the limousine, and I got the up and down look of astonishment.

The man's face asked the question, "where the hell are you from?" The Jamaican hot-dog vendor a few feet away was kind enough to explain to me that the limousine was probably a taxi for rich people. I explained to him that where I was from only the president had a car like that and when he was driving by everyone was supposed to stop and stand still until he passed by. Attempting to move around or continue to walk when the president's limousine was passing could be a sentence for jail time. As I got closer to the YMCA hotel, I saw a family playing music with the father on a keyboard, the mother on guitar, and the children playing percussion with a bowl in front of them to collect donations. Few feet from the musical family I saw a Caucasian man with his daughter eating out of a garbage can. Seeing a Caucasian person eating out of a garbage can on my first day in America, kind of sealed the confusing turmoil in my head and I just had to get back into my room to digest the "load". I watched more TV and went to bed in an American hotel for the first time. It was difficult to turn off the TV because all of a sudden I had control of the TV.

Never in my life had I watched a TV that I had the freedom to change to a different channel. The first time I watched TV was through the holes in the fence of our well to-do neighbor's house. He would put the old black and white TV set on his veranda and the whole neighborhood would line up against his fence starting 8:00PM to view whatever was on from a distance but it was good enough. The TV situation made sense to me when I was told that a Peace Corp volunteer had donated a black and white TV set to the village of Tchiniga during the drilling of the village water well. The simple fact that the TV provided entertainment to the villagers resulted in the birth rate declining 15% the following year. So for those interested in helping third world countries with birth control issues, in my opinion a TV set with a car battery would help the cause also.

After a long day of hard work on the farm and a couple more hours watching TV, everyone would be too tired and forget about sex. I remember when I was about 7 to 8 years of age and we would entertain ourselves by cutting out pictures from magazines. We would tie a white bed sheet between two poles. Then each of us would take turns being the movie producer by holding the cutouts against the white bed sheet lit by a candle or lantern on his side of the sheet. We would move the cutouts against the sheet and tell stories about the pictures. We were watching our own version of TV and it was fun.

On my second day in America, I took a Greyhound bus to Springfield, Massachusetts where the YMCA camp was. When I arrived at the station, a staff member picked me up with a van and took me to the summer camp. I went through the new staff orientation and this session reminded me of the orientation we had been given by the American Cultural Center staff in Lomé. One of the points that were strongly stressed was the warning of committing sexual harassment and rape. We were told that a fourteen-year-old American girl might appear to us as a woman, and to be careful, as the American girls' physical appearance may not match their age. We were told of a case where a Togolese counselor had sex with a girl who he found out later was underage. This counselor was sent back to Togo the very next day.

At this camp in Massachusetts, I was assigned as camp counselor to the youngest group of boys. My roommate was Kpanto, who coincidentally was from Togo as I was. Kpanto was from the north of Togo. For some reason I felt Kpanto did not think I had any business being in America through the same program he was because I was not a traditional English Department student at the University. So from the first day at camp I realized that Kpanto and I could not stand each other. This coupled with the fact that he was from the north and I was from the south of Togo. Unfortunately we brought that ethnic dislike all the way from Africa to the U.S. The fact that we were now in the US, the land of the free; I did not have to worry about Kpanto very much. I took care of my business and let him take care of his.

Two days after the staff orientation, the campers started coming in for a 6 week overnight stay at camp. This camp was primarily for inner city kids from around Springfield, Massachusetts. My cabin was assigned 10 kids ages 6 to 9. Our first breakfast together with the children was an interesting one for me; cereal was passed around and a pint of milk in carton was given to everyone. I never had to handle milk in a carton before. There I was trying my heart out to tear open the rugged rim of the pint of milk. I tried using my hand and then my teeth with no luck. Then little Brian, a 6-year-old boy said to me, "Here Tino, let me show you." He took my pint of milk, spread the angled flat-ends and popped it open effortlessly. It was like magic. I thought to myself at that point that I was in for a "long ride" with this America thing. There were a total of six camp counselors from Africa on the camp and it appeared that we all were more interested in making friends with the American counterparts than with each other. Life on camp was pretty simple; we woke up at the sound of the bugle, assembled at the flagpole for daily announcements, ate breakfast, and then had a day scheduled full of wilderness activities.

Unless a camp counselor had a car, there was nothing around the campsite whatsoever. The camp had a private lake and an island in the middle of the lake. Before I left for the US, to make myself marketable I thought, I went to the neighborhood dance group to learn how to eat fire and how to rub a torch onto my skin without getting burned. Indeed, those skills came in handy at camp when they were telling the Moho Indian story to the children. The Moho story was told around the closing campfire. At the end of the story, Moho was supposed to come out of the lake and run off and disappear into the darkness. Well that year's Moho was coming out of the lake spitting fire. With the help of the American camp staff I adorned an Indian outfit with makeup, feathers and a raffia skirt. When it was time for me to come out, I came out spitting fire and it scared the heck out of the campers. Some remained frightened for up to three days and would not come out of their cabin after dark. The boys' season at the camp was pretty uneventful. At the end of the boys' season, we had an entire weekend off and I managed to setup a meeting with Amelia's parents, who by coincidence lived in a small town in Connecticut only a couple of hours driving distance from where I was. I got to their place on a Friday night and I was nervous. I did not know how they were going to receive me.

Amelia's parents welcomed me into their house and showed me the room where Amelia grew up. They gave me a pair of shorts Amelia's older brother wore when he was a Boy Scout. I stayed at their house overnight and slept in Amelia's old bed. The next morning they took me to breakfast in a dinner they visited for the last 35 years. It was at that dinner where I realized that things would probably not workout between Amelia and me.

When we got to the diner where they were regulars, everyone knew them and now they showed up with a black man.

Everyone was curious and asked them whom did they have the "honor" to meet when they were introduced to me. The father would respond with, "This is Tino. He is an acquaintance of our daughter's in Africa." I felt that this introduction was not a bit to the point. I was their daughter's boyfriend and was living with her, as husband and wife in the Togolese custom, for the last year and a half. At that point, the African in me took over because we believe in Togo that a marriage is not just between a man and a woman, it's between a man and his in-laws as well as between a woman and her in-laws. So that type of introduction of me at the dinner showed me (I thought at that time) that there was no acceptance of me as a potential son-in-law.

Today in 2005, I understand the parent attitude, but then I knew too little of the American culture to understand why they would introduce me as such. They probably did not know the depth of my relationship with their daughter. Over dinner I learned that Amelia's older brother lived in Boston where he was a dancer and the other brother lived in Chicago where he was a physician. Anyway I returned to camp and wished I hadn't ever bothered to meet Amelia's parents. The boys' summer camp season was over and the girls' camp season started. All the American male camp counselors returned to their homes but the African camp counselors were to stay through the girls' season. Female camp counselors came in to replace the male American counselors.

Three days before the girls camp season started there was this beautiful young African-American woman who drove into the camp in a green station wagon. I was sitting on the side of the basketball court playing congas with the camp director's children and when this lady drove up to the camp main office and went inside. After she got out of the office she walked away from the office building to look around the campground. She was wearing a white and orange tie-dye overall with a white t-shirt. This lady put her hand on her hips and looked around. When I noticed her I said to myself, "wow! what a beautiful woman". I later learned that she was one of the female camp counselors who had just arrived from Ohio and would be staying on the camp for the following two weeks.

    Three days later, as the girls' camp season started, I learned that this lady was going to be the head of the female counselors for the next two weeks. At the end of the third day of camp, she was sitting in front of her cabin. Because she was head-counselor, she had her own cabin. I walked up to her and introduced myself. She introduced herself as Abena and said that she was from Cleveland. We talked for a few minutes about how nice the camp was. I was so taken by this woman that I handed her one of the three glass bead bracelets my mother had made for me as things I could sell for money if I needed. I told Abena as I was giving her the bracelet "If I could be married someday, I wished it could be to someone like you." She smiled and did not say a thing. She took the bracelet and put it on right away. My heart melted. I smiled at her and walked away. I was afraid the other American camp staff would suspect I was hitting on her.

    I remembered well the orientation in Africa so I had to be cautious as far as the women were concerned on the campgrounds. From that point on, I had this drive to want to see Abena all the time. I wanted her to see me too and I wanted her to like me. I would wake up about six o'clock in the morning and go swim in the lake hoping that Abena would wake up early also and see me being brave and swimming in the cold lake water. As primal as that feeling was it was real and my time in America started becoming really "meaningful" to me. Abena was teaching the children drama and needed an accompanist drummer. I was fortunate enough to be the drummer/musician among the male staff. I loved seeing her interact with the children. She was kind and respectful to them. The children loved doing the exercises and skits that they wrote with her. It was so wonderful that working with her and the children was like a dream come true.

    All in all I felt very lonely during the girl season, as I was too cautious not to talk to anyone of the female counselors for fear that they may think I was interested in them. On some of my off duty evenings, I took the guitar from the office and went to sit on the deck at the lake and played for hours. It was hard to have an opportunity to speak with Abena as I noticed that all of the

American male camp workers were always around her. She was very kind and courteous with them but showed no interest in them. I knew Abena knew I had a crush on her. Sometimes I would sit and watch her with the children, and she would catch me looking at her and smile back at me. The desire to be with her grew, but the work environment did not allow it very much and my time was running out as the camp season was getting close to the end.

One warm August evening, I was playing guitar on the deck on the lake all alone and I noticed that Abena was in the office area on the computer typing a play that the older girls had written. As I sat at the lake playing, I hoped that somehow she would come to me. At 10:00 p.m. she was done with her typing. She did not go straight to her cabin but heard my guitar and came and sat next to me on the deck. I was still playing the guitar, singing to myself. She said hi, and my heart was pumping so hard. She sat and listened to my music for several minutes.

The moon had risen and was shining on the calm water of the lake. When I finished my song, Abena said to me, "Go get a canoe ready. I'll meet you at the dock in 5 minutes. She went to her cabin and I ran quickly to my cabin and got extra mosquito repellant, as I knew we were going on the island. The canoes were piled up straight against the art & craft building and the art teacher was in there with other counselors working and listening to music. The adrenaline was pumping through me and allowed me to lift the canoe from against the wall without making any noise whatsoever. I gently laid the canoe onto the water. Abena brought two paddles and two life jackets. We put on the life jackets, climbed into the canoe, softly giggling, trying not to make a sound as we took off onto lake.

We were heading to the island, which was about a quarter of a mile offshore. We paddled first with our hands and as we moved farther away from land we started using our paddles. There was a full moon and the sky was perfectly clear. We paddled as quietly as possible to avoid being noticed by the people in the arts and crafts room. We both somehow took our flashlights and when we got on the island, we docked the canoe. As we stood in the shallow water we kissed for the first time. It was like a miracle to me that I was actually kissing such a beautiful woman. I thought I would never stand a chance with her, considering that I was poor and from Africa. Abena told me to collect firewood so we could make a fire. I bravely went in the bushes and collected an armful of dry wood. She took a match out of her pocket and with some dry pine we were able to make a small campfire. We sat and watched the fire for several minutes and talked a little about ourselves. She looked at me over the flames, and my heart skipped a beat. She stood up and took our 2 jackets and made a make shift mat. She took my hand and led me to the mat and then kissed me gently.

We made a passionate love for a long time right under the watchful eyes of the full moon. It was like a fairy tale. We both wanted that moment to last as long as possible but because we had to be on duty the following day, we packed our stuff and got back in the canoe to return to the camp ground around 3:00 am. We returned to shore as quietly as we took off. The next morning I missed my show off swimming in the lake session for Abena. I was too tired to wake up early that morning. Now the excitement was doubled. I could not wait to see her, I was falling in love, I thought.

Then I received a post card mailed from New York City two days later. The post card was from Amelia who said on the card that someone was coming to the U.S. from Togo and she asked the person to mail the postcard once they were in the U.S. That was common practice, as people in Togo would go to the airport with their letters to their relatives and beg the travelers to mail the letter once they reached Europe. That was one sure way of knowing that the letter would get to the destination. So I was not surprised by that post card. On the Post card Amelia wrote that she hoped that I was doing okay and having a good time in America. She was still looking for jobs and said that there was a strong possibility that she might get an offer with the Republic of Benin's office of USAID (United States Agency for International Development) organization. The camping season was getting close to the end and it became very difficult for Abena and me to hook up. That created a greater need in me to want to talk to her and to be with her. One day, during a rainstorm, I stopped by Abena's cabin to say hello. She greeted me at the door and invited me in. Once I was in the cabin, she looked in my eyes and told me how beautiful they were. Once again, passion struck and we made love in her cabin to the sound of rain gently tapping on the roof. Our reality was clear, we all were going back to where we came from and resume our previous lives.

    I was returning to Africa at the end of the summer and Abena was going back to Cleveland, Ohio. The day before she left the campgrounds for Ohio, she found me to tell me how sorry she was and that we were going to need to leave things "as is" with no promises.

    I cried at the thought that somehow this woman that at first I thought I did not stand a chance with, actually made passionate love to me and now she was telling me goodbye. The day before she left, I helped her wash and prepare her car. As she drove off of the campgrounds, I stood next to an ancient pine tree and cried. As she drove past me, I could see she was crying as well.

eibBooks.com
As in Electronic Instant Books
As in eXcellence In Book Selling

Get your book published online instantly, electronically and/or in paperback format like this book and sell it directly on Zongo*Me*.com

We show you how!

CHAPTER SEVEN

*M*y camp counselor engagement was over and the YMCA had planned to provide the International camp counselors with the opportunity to see the country. The International camp counselors were randomly grouped for various tour routes. There was a tour that went to Atlanta, and one to Washington D. C., and the last one to Chicago, Illinois. Fortunately I was put on the Chicago, Illinois tour. That meant I would take the Greyhound bus from New York City to Chicago where a local YMCA coordinator would pick me up at the Greyhound station in Chicago. We would be placed with a host family where we would spend the nights and the YMCA van would take us to see the city during the days. We were to spend four days in Chicago. I was informed that I was going to spend two days with a female school teacher who volunteered to host me for two nights and two days with a family of four before returning to Washington D.C., then back to New York and off to Togo.

Since I learned from Amelia's parents that Amelia's brother was living in Chicago, I called for his telephone number and hoped to be able to meet with him and his pregnant wife, so at least I could say to Amelia when I got back to Togo that I met her parents and her brother. Meanwhile, my Greyhound bus ride surprisingly had to go through Cleveland, Ohio where Abena had returned. I arrived at the Greyhound station in Cleveland around 6:15 am on a Saturday. I was so excited, and hope that I could invite Abena to come to see me at the bus station for few minutes before my next leg of the trip resumed. When I called her place, she picked up the phone and seemed annoyed that I called that early in the morning. She told me she could not talk to me at that moment because her boyfriend was asleep in her bedroom. I was crushed and did not know what to do. I needed to get my mind ready to prepare for my graduation exams in Togo so I tried to distract myself from all the stress of having met Abena. I tried to forget about the uncomfortable situation with Amelia's parents and now Abena wouldn't even talk to me and there I was possibly going to meet with Amelia's brother. I felt guilty. I felt I had cheated on Amelia and thought I deserved all the mistreatment I was getting from Abena. When I got to Chicago, the YMCA van was indeed there with Andrew the chauffeur. Andrew took me to my host person who was an older female high school teacher. At my host house, I called Amelia's brother's house to try and make an arrangement to meet with them. When I called, his "wife" picked up the phone or so I thought. I set up an appointment to meet with Luke's wife in front of the Sears' tower at 2:00 PM the next day so she could take me to their house and I could spend some time with them. The next day we went on our morning tour, which ended at the Sears tower where I requested to be dropped off. We were a bit late getting to the Sears tower. I was nervous and smoked two cigarettes wondering if Luke and his wife would view me as their potential brother-in-law or not. I stood on the sidewalk in front of the Sears tower looking around for a woman who might seem to be looking for someone.

Around 2:15 PM, I felt a tap on my right shoulder and when I turned to the right to see who that could be, I could not see anyone. Then I turned to the left and guess who was there with a bouquet of flowers in her hand? It was Amelia holding a bouquet of flowers she brought for me! This could not be, I thought. She was supposed to be in Africa, not in Chicago, so I freaked out, and I was shouting, "Oh my god, oh my god!" Amelia was laughing her pants off at the expression of disbelief in my face. I was scared and could not believe what I had in front of me, so I would touch her arm several times to confirm that I was touching a real human.

When I was growing up, there had been stories I overheard grownups talked about such as when a person dies, his or her spirit can manifest at different places as an in person character to the loved ones. In my panic, I thought, I hope Amelia had not died in Togo waiting for me while I was in America, now that her soul was manifesting itself to me.

My heart was pounding and Amelia would not stop laughing. She eventually took me to a small bar where we sat and I asked her what in the world was she doing in Chicago Illinois? Amelia said she needed me to guess why she was here. I thought something might have been wrong with her parents who were both senior citizens, she responded negative. I thought something was wrong with her brother and his wife. I thought she got a job offer and she could not wait. All my attempts to guess the reason why the lady I left in Africa would be in Chicago were not successful. So she had to explain to me why she was in America all together. Amelia asked me if I remembered when we made love without using a condom the last night before I left for America. I responded yes and she continued to tell me that she got pregnant. She went on further to explain that since it was my decision to come to America to participate in the exchange program with the YMCA, she felt it was her choice to decide what was right for her body thus she came to America to have an abortion. Her brother Luke who was a physician paid her way back to the U.S. to have the abortion. I could not believe what I was hearing.

    She mentioned that she was the one who mailed the post card from New York to me at camp. She added that she did not want to ruin my good time at camp. As I was listening to this story, my emotions went from anger to disgust. So I asked Amelia, why was she telling me all this, if she felt it was not necessary to tell me about it before she got the abortion. Her response was that she was going to tell me eventually anyway.

    The day we met in Chicago was her last day in Chicago and she was returning to Togo to wait for me till I got back. Remember, that I was put on the tour route to Chicago by pure chance; I could have been on the tour that went to Atlanta. I thought to myself, had I had enough money to pay for her way to the U.S. to have the abortion she would have given me the courtesy of informing me. I wondered if I was the real author of the pregnancy and that perhaps she had taken another lover. Amelia expected me to feel sorry for her about all she went through. Unfortunately no part of me could feel any pity for her, I was rather angry at her for not even thinking I was worth the courtesy of knowing that I fathered a child. Right there it was clear to me that our relationship was doomed, compounded by the simple fact that I allowed myself to fall in love with Abena at camp and ultimately by this act by her. Amelia further explained that when I called the brother's house the night before and spoke to the wife, in fact I was speaking to her. Amelia informed me that she had received a job offer in Benin and that she was going to travel to Benin to check out the position once she returned to Togo. This meant that there was a chance that she might not have been there in Lomé when I got back to Togo if I hadn't come to Chicago to find out her plans. We had a late lunch and a couple of beers and went to her brother's house where I met her brother and his real wife.

    Everything went pretty cool, at the brother's despite the fact that I was brewing inside, confused and angry. I thought I lost everything and that my trip to America was not ending happily as I would have hoped. Luke and his wife were cool, and treated me with respect but I could not be sure if they knew I was the author of the pregnancy they just helped Amelia terminate. The issue never came up and I would not want to discuss it anyway as I was angry at him also for having paid Amelia's way to the U.S. to have an abortion without at least informing me of the situation and getting my opinion on the matter. I was taken back to my host family late in the night in the brother's convertible Porsche with the top down.

    I left Chicago the next day and went to spend the night with a host family in Indiana. This host family had two daughters age 14 and 17. After dinner, the daughters asked their father if they could rent a movie to watch with me. We went to the movie rental place and they checked out the movie titled "Coming to America" where Eddie Murphy was the star. After the movie, my host family all laughingly asked me whether I was a real life prince like the one Eddie Murphy depicted in the movie. I told them no, that my coming to America was only because I could speak English and did well on the proficiency test. The host family thought I kind of looked like Eddy Murphy and they wanted me to try to laugh like him, and when I did, they all "fell off" their seat in amazement at how even close my laughing was to Eddy Murphy's. I continued to entertain, talk with them about my life in Africa, and laugh even though my heart felt like crying. I left Indiana in route to Washington DC where the tour took me to the Smithsonian Museum, and the White House. Visiting the White House was a very powerful experience to me. Being at the house where President Reagan, who I used to watch on ABC News at the American cultural center in Togo with so much admiration, was a moving experience to me. I only dreamed of one day coming to this country and perhaps see President Reagan speak in person, and here I was actually standing in the house where he lived and led the country. I bought a lot of postcards from the White House that I hoped to show people back home to prove to them that I actually was in the White House.

At the Smithsonian museum, I saw moon rocks and several other amazing things. It was here that I met Toni, an African-American girl with blond hair, who was working at the museum and guarding the moon rock. I did not know that some African-American women were borne with blond hair. As I was asking Tony questions about the moon rock, she realized I was from Africa and she started asking questions about me and where I was from. After having been so depressed about my lost love with Abena, who did not feel there was any future for us and Amelia, who had just aborted my child without telling me, I kind of let this lady at the Smithsonian flirt with me, as I needed a friend. Toni asked questions about Togo and Africa in general. I believe now that she probably had watched the Eddie Murphy movie as well because her questions indicated to me that she was trying to find out if I was from a rich African family. She jokingly offered to marry me for $10,000. I did not understand what she meant until I actually returned to America the second time and found out that some people pay to marry an American woman in order to stay in this country, thus which explained why Toni mentioned $10,000.

Before I left the Smithsonian museum, Toni invited me to a nightclub named The Kilimanjaro that night. I was excited that she invited me to a club. In Washington DC, the camp counselors stayed at a youth housing building where everyone had to be back by 10:00 p.m. because the gates were closed at that time. I was to take the taxi to the Kilimanjaro nightclub to meet Toni and her sister. I got to the Kilimanjaro early enough so as not to miss the opportunity to get some female attention that I needed so desperately. Toni and her older sister looked fabulous. By the time I got to Washington DC, the $250.00 stipend I got from working at the summer camp was getting really low and I had $10.00 in my pocket that night after paying for my ride to the club. Very soon I realized that Toni and her sister were expecting me to pay their way into this club, which was $15.00 per person. I did not even have enough money to cover myself and I knew all the way from Togo that one had to take care of oneself as far as going out was concerned, so I figure, $10.00 would be enough to cover me and that Toni and her sister would pay their own way to the club and we would have a good time.

To my embarrassment, I found out that Toni and her sister, even though they were "dressed to kill," had no money in their pockets and were hoping that I was going to take care of them at this club. Since I did not know what to do as far as nightclubs were concerned in the U.S., I just stood there and hoped that the girls would manage to get us in. Finally they saw someone they knew and they got us in. I only had to pay out my $10.00 and they got in free. In my mind, I was behaving in the "American way" taking care of myself with my money to pay my own way. But I realized that the girls were disappointed and disgusted with me and thought I was some cheap "MF". They let me know that soon enough because once inside the club, Toni ignored me as if she had never met me before. I thought this night was going to boost my self-esteem a bit but to the contrary, it kind of confirmed to me that I just was not worth anything to any American woman period! I was hurt and I tried to dance my hurt away but looked more pathetic on the dance floor as I was dancing by myself while Toni and her sister were doing the lambada with other guys they might have known.

I did not even have a ride back to my place and because it was passed 10:00 p.m., I had nowhere to go until the next day. My options were clear that night, I could act really hurt and end up wandering the streets of Washington D.C. all night until the next day or I could play it cool and hopefully Toni and sister would be kind enough to take me with them. I played it cool, I put my ego "in my pocket and sat on it". Around 2:00 am when the club was closing, Toni came to say good night to me and I told her that I had no place to go as I had no money to return home. She felt sorry for me and asked her sister if they could take me to their apartment. As we were going to their apartment, the fantasy part of my male ego went wild in my head, I hoped that the girls would have a change of heart and maybe I would experience the wildest moment in my life in a threesome.

At their apartment, Toni gave me a glass of water that I asked for and handed me a blanket. She then showed me the love seat in the living room, which was going to be my bed that night. Although it was not a full couch, I was grateful; it was better than walking in the city to kill time till the next day when the youth hostel would be open. The next day seemed too long to come as the love seat was uncomfortable and falling asleep was also impossible due to the anticipation of the possibility that somehow they would invite me in for some wild adventure.

The next morning, Toni made some toast and gave me tea, and I was grateful. Toni and her sister took me in her car back to the youth hostel where they simply dropped me off. Toni gave me her address and her phone number, which I later found out were false. I was ready to go back to Togo. Still part of me would like to have been able to stay with Abena. Andrew the head camp counselor coordinator in Chicago gave me his calling card numbers so I could use it to make any call in the US if I needed, so I tried a couple of times to contact Abena. I reached her once, but she reiterated that she was involved with someone else. I was certain my relationship with Amelia was going to the tube. I prayed that somehow Abena would have a change of heart, after all, she gave me the greatest sexual experience in my life, making love in the middle of the night under the full moon light on an island, just the two of us. I did not think anything could top that experience, thus deep in my heart I was falling in love even though I knew I could not be with her. She did make it clear with words that she was not interested, and that she was involved with someone else.

While sitting on the grass in the mall area in DC watching all the tourists walking around on that hot summer day, I prayed to God to allow me to come back to this country. I said to myself in an audible voice "I want to come back to this country", "I need to come back to this country."

I was an emotional wreck at this time and I needed to take the bus to New York City and get ready to go back to Africa. When I arrived in New York City, I took the ferry to the Ellis Island to see the Statue of Liberty. After reading about the story of the statue, I got in line to climb the steps to the top of the statue. Again, I felt full emotionally like I felt while in the White House. Tears came to my eyes again as I felt deeply that I had touched FREEDOM, and yet I was going back to Africa where I could not dare talk politics whatsoever. I could clearly say I was truly bitten by the freedom bug and there was no turning back. I will have freedom I said. At the top of the Statue of liberty, I felt the chill once more and the tears fell again, it was a silent cry for the God of FREEDOM to claim me as "one of his". I came down from the statue and right there I saw two lives in front of me: My life of poverty that I was returning to (I was supposed to be studying for the final exam I was to take when I got back) and the life of NOW, poor but FREE. I could see the potential for all the things I could do in this country. I could be anything in this country. I asked myself, how I could have been so close to the best possible opportunity for me and yet have to simply return to a land where there was only opportunity for those who were related to or in the same tribe as the president.

I saw other tourists were throwing pennies in the jar at the foot of the Statue of Liberty, I took out some coins and I was not going to just toss my coins, I was going to ask the spirit of the Statue of Liberty to help me come back just like the young man from UCLA did in the village in Africa when he prayed to get accepted on his college's basketball team. So I held the coins to my mouth and ask the spirit of the Statue of Liberty to please bring me back to this country and I tossed the coins. From that very moment, I felt as if the statue had accepted my request and I had the feeling of hope inside me. I just knew it was there.

I got back to the YMCA motel on Sloan Avenue in New York where all the international camp counselors had returned and were preparing themselves to return to their respective home countries. This place was packed with young people just full of energy and all type of characters. I was to fly out the following day to get back to Togo. We all stayed up in the lounge talking and sharing our experiences. All of a sudden, somehow, there was this girl from the Midwest who was on her way to New York University who took interest in me and wanted to sleep with me. After all that I had been through emotionally, I said to myself, "What the heck." We went to my room to have sex and used the last condom I had. She wanted to continue and I had to run out of my hotel room to bang on the doors of the other international counselors asking them if they had a spare condom. Unfortunately the five doors that I knocked on, the occupants, besides telling me that they did not have any "spare condoms", as if they would have given it to me anyway, laughed at me. The STUPID self-destructive instinct in me once again said, "What a heck", and I went on and had unprotected sex with someone I just met the same day. PLEASE, DO NOT MAKE THE SAME MISTAKE I MADE, IT IS NOT WORTH IT.

Although the one-nightstand moment was great and boosted my ego, I spent the rest of the night worrying about the possibility that I might have just contacted aids. The fear stayed with me for a long time and it negated all the thrill of having had a one-nightstand. So do not do it!

eibBooks.com
As in Electronic Instant Books
As in eXcellence In Book Selling

Get your book published online instantly, electronically and/or in paperback format like this book and sell it directly on Zongo*Me*.com

We show you how!

The Way It Was *Coming To America:* The Real Story.

PART THREE

Returning to Africa the First Time

CHAPTER EIGHT

*O*n the plane back to Africa, I tried to study for my finals but I could not concentrate at all. I was going back to the life I thought I left behind with Amelia but somehow that life had all kinds of twists to it. I was lost; I did not want to face Amelia, part because I felt humiliated by her decision to have the abortion, and because of the guilt I felt for having gotten involved sexually with two women while I was in America, one of which I had fallen in love with. Unfortunately the African man in me could not accept the fact that the woman who was by all definitions and customs, my wife, could make a decision as serious as aborting my child without telling me. In reality, I had no job, but my mother and sisters would have loved to take my child if Amelia and I could not raise the child. I felt that we could have made it anyway with a child. I would have done anything to help raise my child. The fact that she did not trust me with this responsibility and honor put an end to our relationship.

As mentioned previously, prior to my trip to America, Amelia and I were living together as Togolese husband and wife. She came to meet me at the airport but I felt no excitement when I saw her. I wished she had not come. I wished she had accepted the job in Benin that she was going to be checking out without telling me. So we rode the taxi together to the house. I could not touch her; I could not look at her in the face. I was mad at her and mad at myself because of the guilt I had for having gotten her pregnant and leaving. Amelia, cried, and asked me to forgive her for what she had done. She had even gone to talk to my mother and sisters to come to plea with me to forgive her. Obviously she did not tell them the exact reason why she needed me to forgive her. She just told them that she had made a big mistake. The feelings I had for her were just not there any more. After two weeks, I decided to go find my own place to live. I felt that I could not continue to depend on her to pay for my lodging and food while I could not stand her for what she had done, and I could not stand myself for what I had done. I was too much "a man" to forgive myself and forgive her, and go on trying to rebuild our life together. I found a small one-room apartment on an empty lot attached to someone's house to rent. It was close enough to the University that I could walk to school. I helped Amelia find a small apartment and helped her move. We tried to use sex as a cure for our problems but it did not work. It did not heal the hurt that was still there. It was up to me to cut off the relationship or to make it work. I chose to cut it loose for fear that if I stayed with her and we had face other life challenges I would not be able to trust her to make the decisions that would be in our best interest.

On two occasions, before I went to the U.S., during arguments she would say to me that the only reason I wanted to be with her was so I could come to America, because, that was what all the men she got involved with while a Peace Corp volunteer wanted out of her. That really annoyed me. I had managed to visit America on my own, and I was gone for three months. In my mind I had created a better future for myself by improving my English and widening my horizons. I thought I had proven to her that I was not one of those "other" African men, and that I actually loved her. Her actions coupled with my own confirmed to me that it was the end of our relationship. That was the end of Amelia and me.

I continued with my studies at the University and because I came to America the year before, my Archaeology professor who was going to the University of Ibadan in Nigeria for the International Conference of Archaeologists and Africanists, asked if I would be interested in going to Nigeria with her to serve as her interpreter. I said yes and off to Nigeria we went. There was a Togolese driver, my professor, another guy as a bodyguard and myself as the translator. This was the first time I was going to Nigeria. In my language Nigeria was called "Anoli" which literally means dead man. It was a common perception that if anyone was venturing into Nigeria his parents or family might as well already start his or her funeral. Nigeria is a highly populated country and supposedly a place with a high crime rate according to stories reported back to Togo back then. So I was nervous about going to Nigeria with my Professor, but the privilege of having been asked by my University to perform this service outweighed the fear.

We did not have a hard time going through the military checkpoints because our car's license plate was one issued by the Togolese government. We were on "official business" thus did not have to pay all the tips the commercial transportation drivers unofficially had to pay the machine-gun bearing soldiers. The trip all the way to Lagos was uneventful. From Lagos to the State of Ibadan was an eye-opener experience about the reality of life in of Nigeria. There were a lot of people indeed, and traffic was very congested. I saw a lot of American yellow school buses that were being used as public transportation. They were full of passengers to the point that that the last passenger to get on board would only hang on the steps with the risk of falling. Despite the reports that Nigeria was so crowded that when a pedestrian was hit by a car, other cars just kept on going and the cadaver would get flattened on the ground, I did not see any dead people being continuously run over by other cars. We got to Ibadan by the end of the day and checked into a small hotel near the University where the conference was to take place.

The conference started on a Monday and the first day was dedicated to introductions of all the participants and the chance to get acquainted with the various sites that were hosting the conference. I sat next to my professor all through the meetings and had a note pad on which I wrote down notes to assist me with my translation. I tried to whisper the translation into my professor's ear but it became obvious that it would not work that way, so quickly I had to improvise. As I was listening to the presenters speak in English, I would write down on my note pad in French the translation as fast as I could and she would read from my notepad. After a while this method proved to be the best way; it got easier for me as I started to use shorthand writing that I used while taking courses at the University in Togo.

The first day of the conference went very well and we went back to the hotel, changed our clothes, and went down to the restaurant. I shared the room with our driver and the bodyguard. After dinner we went down to the main lobby where we could hang out and were served beer. Two foreigners were also lodging at the hotel, one was an American guy who was doing field research on education and the other was a Swiss lady who had just completed her research on deforestation in Nigeria. The next day during lunch at the conference, I met a beautiful Nigerian student named Ife who was studying to become a French teacher. Ife showed interest in me and so did I in her. We spoke French and it was great to see such a beautiful African woman actually interested in me. We saw each other every day during lunch break and were fond of each other. I explained to Ife how I got to Ibadan and that I hoped to return to America some day. Everyday of our stay at the hotel, we hung-out at the lobby after dinner, and got to know the American guy and the Swiss Lady. The American guy's name was Ahcas and the Swiss lady's name was Suzie.

The last day of the conference, I did not see Ife during our lunchtime routine and I was crushed; the only thing I knew of her was the school's department office where I met her so we could have lunch. I went to the Language Department office and asked people if they had seen her. No one could help me and nobody knew where she could be found. It was not like everyone had a telephone in their house so I could just call the telephone directory to inquire about Ife. I was devastated and could not say goodbye to Ife. Nevertheless, our "new American and Swiss friends" were there when we were leaving and as a custom, I said to them, "you know you have a friend in Togo now, whenever you are in Togo, do not hesitate to contact me, you have a place to stay". I drew a map to where I was living then in Togo on a piece of notebook paper that I handed to both of them.

Our ride back to Lomé was not fast enough. The whole way back I kept thinking about how I was going to return to Ibadan by myself to find Ife. I was not scared anymore now that I did not see any of the atrocities in Nigeria that my culture had so cruelly and wrongfully reported. It got totally dark when we got back to Lagos and as we were in the middle lane of the road, two big school busses were on each side of our car at the traffic light. For the first time, I experienced the illusion of driving backward, when the buses on each side of us started to move forward before our car, our driver panicked and screamed and slammed on his brake saying his car was moving backward. It was the first time in his life driving on a multi-lane highway. We got to Lome very late in the night and on the following Monday, my professor gave me 10,000 cfa, which is about $20.00 in payment for my translation job. I was happy for the money and for the opportunity.

eibBooks.com
As in Electronic Instant Books
As in eXcellence In Book Selling

Get your book published online instantly, electronically and/or in paperback format like this book and sell it directly on Zongo*Me*.com

We show you how!

CHAPTER NINE

*T*he following Wednesday, I set out to Ibadan, now that I sort of knew the way there. I needed to see Ife to say goodbye and hopefully to see where her heart was before we said goodbye. Somehow I kept finding myself attracted to women I could not possibly "have". I got to Ibadan, by early afternoon and rushed to the Department of Languages on the campus and looked for Ife to no avail, no one knew her whereabouts nor could they help me find her. So I stayed there, wandered around hopelessly and eventually accepted that she probably did not want to see me. I went to the bus station and took a truck back to Lagos and then a station wagon to Lomé. My heart was broken but what could I do, I needed to get back to Lome and get ready to go to school. I had already skipped school to return to Ibadan to try to find Ife.

Meanwhile, classes at the University went on uneventfully. Sometimes on my way back to the campus I would ride my moped by Amelia's new house to see if she was there, as part of me at times still needed to know she was doing well. My heart was crushed when once I saw a Rasta man and her hugging in front of her house as I rode my bike by. Then I realized for sure, I was the one who did not want her any longer and that I should not expect her to wait for me forever.

I wrote a letter to Abena in America to express to her that I really would like her to reconsider her position as far as we were concerned. I truly believed that we could have something special together. She replied to me asking me to give it a rest and that she was involved with someone and not to bother her any longer.

After three months, I was studying together with my college buddy Tsphore behind the local post office and for the "millionth" time I went to check my mailbox and this time there was something in it from America. It was a telegram from Abena; the message read: "Dear Tino, I realized that I made a terrible mistake the way I treated you. I hope you forgive me for mistreating you. I would like you to come now to be with me". As I was reading this telegram, I could not believe my eyes; I showed the telegram to my buddy Tsphore to read. I thought this woman must be out of her mind, and why did I have to receive this telegram at this moment in my life when I needed to concentrate for my mid-term examination. I had just started to work out of my mind the whole Ife situation. I guess I need to get excited, after all it was the best news I had heard in the last three months. It was like a dream come true.

I went around asking "anyone and their mother" if they could help me make a phone call to the U.S. without having to pay because I did not have any money. I wrote a lot of letters to Abena and sometimes got lucky and was able to talk to her on the phone. I started tutoring for English and when I got paid, I bought Kente cloth backpacks and sent them to Abena in Cleveland to sell them and hopefully by the time I wanted to go back to the U.S. to be with her she would have enough money to help me with my plane ticket. Now that Abena wanted me to come to join her, I sent another letter to the summer camp where we met the previous year stating my desire to rejoin them again the coming summer as a camp counselor. I also sent my resume to other camps in America as a backup plan just in case my original camp did not respond to me. I never received a letter of acknowledgement of my letter of intention from the previous summer camp. Abena now sent me love letters with her pictures to help me cope with the separation. I wrote a letter to her every week to report to her what was going on in my life.

One hot afternoon, I was returning from the campus to my house and to my surprise in front of the gate there was Suzie the Swiss lady I met at the hotel in Nigeria. She was standing in front of my house with her bicycle and her suitcases. She followed the map I drew on the notebook sheet of paper to come to my house. What was this, I wondered? Was God trying to play some sort of trick on me? So we gave each other hugs and kisses of welcome as the Europeans do. We walked to my place which was no more that a 7'x7' small room that I was renting from a lady landlord. The room had a corrugated iron roof and a small window way up close to the ceiling to prevent potential thieves from entering the room. It was hot in my room but I had an old electric fan someone gave me. The fan had no protective grills and I had to hold it in place with a pile of books otherwise it could walk across the room. Suzie said, since I said she was welcome whenever she was in Togo, she decided to visit Togo on her way back to Switzerland. She wanted to know if she could spend two weeks with me to check out the city of Lome before she went back home. I said sure (since in my culture, one is to treat the stranger with kindness since one does not know when he/she would be a stranger in another's country).

Now, there I was with a woman in my house all of a sudden! I did the cooking for lunch and dinner. We shared the same bed and the first couple of nights were cordial with no sexual intentions expressed either way. I told Suzie that I had a girlfriend in America and that the next time I went to America, I would not come back to Togo and that I would join my girlfriend in Ohio. We talked and really became real close. Everyday when I went to my classes, Suzie would ride her bicycle to the downtown where she would hangout until the end of the day. Sometimes she came to see me and we would have lunch together at the house. It was nice. After a week, I discovered that Suzie found a bar at the beach owned by a Togolese man and his French wife, and that she got "high" there every time she went to town. I was disappointed about that fact, but she was a free woman. In my culture we believe that when someone smokes "Gué", that's what we call marijuana, the person would eventually go crazy. I was disappointed that my new friend would do something like that especially remembering my own experience with drugs.

When I was in tenth grade, I came to Lome for summer vacation and was staying with my friends as my mother was living too far from the city. I went to visit a school friend of mine that I knew from Atakpame where I was going to high school. This friend and his family lived very close to the border of Ghana, the country west of Togo. My friend, and his other buddy decided to walk across the border into Ghana to go visit a friend I did not really know but I needed their company so I was invited to go. When we got there it was a very hot day and the supposed friend we were visiting in Ghana was actually an older married guy with his wife and child. They lived in a shack made of woven coconut branches.

I noticed immediately that something was wrong with their child's face. The child had a very deformed skull and his eyes were very close together, some sort of birth defect. We went through the greetings and then my friend asked the man if he had some "fire"? I wondered what he could mean by some "fire" as sometimes we referred to cigarettes as "fire" in the youth slang. Then I thought we wouldn't have done all that walking across a machine gun-guarded border just for some cigarettes. The man said yes of course and brought out a tin container. He tore up a cement package paper and poured a handful of some dried herb onto the sheet of paper. My friend took it and gave him seventy-five francs, about fifteen cents U.S. My friend rolled up the herb into the piece of the cement package paper and sealed it using his saliva.

The cigarette he just made was as fat as an adult's thumb. He lit it and drew some deep puffs and handed it to his friend who drew some deep puffs and passed this fat cigarette to me. I did as they did since I was a cigarette smoker at that time. I drew some deep puffs and passed it back to the first one that started the round.

When it came back to me the second time, I already knew I had enough and that the thing I just smoked was no ordinary cigarette. I started feeling weird. All of a sudden, I realized I must have smoked "Gué". I started to get scared that I was going to go crazy. When my two companions finished with the fat cigarette, we decided to return to Togo. As we started to walk back to Togo, my body became polarized - and that is the best way I could describe the sensation inside of me. When the wind blew my shirt against my chest if felt like the fire sparks from two electrical wires touching each other. The burning sensation of sparks on my chest became unbearable to the point that I had to unbutton my shirt and hold each side away from my skin to keep it from touching me. I could not keep my lips together as doing so created a shocking electrical feeling on them so I walked with my mouth opened all the way back to my friend's place in Togo.

The incredible sensation got worse as we were getting closer to his house. Now even my blood started to feel like fire circulating inside my body. I could then feel my blood going through every vein in my body. I felt I just needed to lie down and as soon as we got to the house, I ran to their living room to lie on the floor and took off the shirt that was "burning" my skin. There was a small radio playing music in the living room. I felt like I was inside of the radio and imagined all the mechanisms inside of the radio and could even go inside the parts on the circuit board of the radio. The thought that I, the "son of my mother" had just smoked marijuana was terrifying. I felt awful and ashamed of myself for not living up to my mother's expectations. I prayed that I did not become a crazy person, as becoming crazy was what was eventually expected from someone who smokes "Gué".

After we ate, and a lot we ate, I started to feel slowly like myself again. I left my friend's house around 5:00 p.m. and walked the five miles back home. I never wanted to see this friend who introduced me to this stuff. I swore to myself never to smoke marijuana again. So when I found out that my new friend Suzie was going downtown to smoke this stuff, I was disappointed, but figured she would be going back to Switzerland shortly and thus did not make a big deal out of it.

One afternoon, I received a letter from a summer camp in the U.S. with an offer inviting me to join their staff for the coming summer. The camp in Connecticut was willing to pay my way from Paris to New York where their van would pick me up and take me to Connecticut. I was excited and yet depressed because I did not know how in the world I was going to make my way to Paris. As I was laying down under the Mango tree trying not to be too depressed, Suzie returned home to meet me for lunch. She walked her bicycle into the yard and saw me lying down. She came and sat next me and we greeted each other. She noticed immediately that something was wrong. When she asked me what was wrong, I told her that I just got another job offer from the U.S. but that I needed to pay my way to Paris before the camp would pay my way to New York. To my surprise, Suzie said that she would be able to help me when she got back to Switzerland. I thought to myself, that this woman had only known me for a month and why would she possibly want to help me! In any case, my worries about being able to get to Paris were somewhat alleviated. We continued living together and finally our relationship grew more intimate.

Everything I knew about making love was "getting in" there and doing it as hard as you could. Suzie became my teacher and I am grateful. The first time Suzie and I were to make love; I was doing the caressing and wanted to get busy right away. She looked at me straight in the eyes with her beautiful big eyes and said "take your time, you are not a tiger and this is not a pray that you have to catch to survive, take your time, take it slow". That was the first time I heard of such a concept as far as sex was concerned. After all, my sexual education was from the few porn movies and magazines I saw. So I did take it slow, making more use of my hands. When eventually we connected, everything was just right, I could feel it and the pleasure was wonderful and mutual. I learned through Suzie that making love has many dimensions, and that the more time I took engaging my woman the more pleasure I gave, and the more pleasure I got. Suzie left me two weeks later for Switzerland and I was grateful for the lessons she taught me, for her friendship and for the hope she instilled in me by offering to help me financially with my trip to Paris and eventually to the U.S.

School was going well, June approached, and it became a bit difficult to concentrate on my studies as I was preoccupied with how was I going to find money to pay for my plane ticket to Paris. Two weeks before the deadline for showing the Camp Counselor Program coordinator that you have secured a plane ticket, I got a notice from the postal office that there was a certified letter waiting for me. I rushed to the post office and received an international money order in the amount of $2,000.00 from Suzie with a note that when I got to the U.S., and got a job, I could pay her back. I could not believe it. It was a miracle for me as far as I was concerned. My family could not have assisted me financially to purchase a plane ticket that cost $1000.00.

I rushed to Air Afrique to purchase my plane ticket, which I needed, to be able to receive my visa to the U.S. When I got to the Embassy and actually got the visa stamped onto my passport, I could not believe what was going on for me. My life was changing in front of my own eyes. I knew I was not coming back to Africa, but I could not tell anyone that truth; even my mother and the rest of my family did not know that I was not coming back. I did not tell my mother because; I was her only son that she took away from the catholic school when she heard that I was showing interest in becoming a priest. I felt that telling her would have broken her heart because her only son was going so far and she would not have the chance to arrange a marriage for him, as she would wish. Part of me also was afraid that had she known, she would have gone to the village and ask one of my uncles to do some voodoo that would somehow prevent me from living.

CHAPTER TEN

*I*n May I took my final exam at the University and not to my surprise, I found out that I did not pass my graduation exam. Under normal circumstances, I would have another chance in September to take the exam again, but who would give up the opportunity to come to America for a chance to take an examination that you knew you were sure to fail. So to America I was going with an extra $1,000.00 in my pocket. I went to the Grand Marché (downtown marketplace) and bought artifacts and African clothes, which I knew I could sell once in the U.S. to make extra money.

Since Abena sent me the telegram to "come now", I was ready to come to America. Knowing that I was coming to the U.S. for good, I told my college band members about my situation and we decided to record a demo tape of one of the songs I wrote with the hope that once in America, I could find a producer that would be interested in the song. The song was my call to the African people to wake up and take responsibility for our lives by being creative in thinking about ways to solve our problems. I implored the creativity within all of us to wake up and do something. What prompted me to write the song was what I saw as the lack of drive in the youth at the time. We were kind of left on our own and we simply wandered around with no direction from one day to another. I saw our people's energy not being optimized to improve our lives in Africa so I was calling on people to see that a whole lot could be changed in our lives if we just did something.

Should you want to listen to the song you may pay me $2.50 to listen to it by connecting to the Internet an login onto http://www.ZongoMe.com/ListenLive/
I will give $1.00 to charity to help feed the less fortunate and the balance to pay for the hosting services where the song resides at this moment. If you would like to have an album of songs that I recorded with my group on an autographed CD mailed to you, logon to: ZongoMe.com/AutographedCD. The autographed CD of the song will cost you $12.00 of which $4.00 will be given to charity to help feed the less fortunate.

To prepare for my final departure from Togo, I sold my books, my chair and study table, my "walking dangerous electrical fan", my hand-made guitar and everything else of "value" I had except a small Casio synthesizer keyboard someone gave me that I thought was so sophisticated that I might not be able to find same kind in America. I was determined to bring that keyboard with me to America.

When it was time to leave Togo, my mother and three sisters and a couple of friends came to send me off. I had a big duffel bag full of stuff, my carry-on bag and my keyboard. Giving hugs and kisses was not something we did a lot of in my family, thus the separation was uneventful. I gave my mother and sisters a hug and told them see you later. This time I was not scared of flying when the plane took off from Lomé. Since I was going for good, I needed to prepare for the American life thus I went to the flea market and bought me a leather jacket that was sort of orange in color.

I decided to stain that leather to kind of revive its color a bit. Since I could not find a good leather stain, I bought burgundy shoe polish and polished the jacket. But I guess one was not supposed to use shoe polish to stain a leather jacket as my jacket started to smell really bad. I thought hanging the jacket in the sun would enable the wax to melt into the leather so when I buffed it, it would look nice and the smell would go away. Well, the smell did not go away and now I had a streaked jacket as a result of applying the shoe polish unevenly. I would not give up so I bought aerosol deodorant and seriously sprayed my jacket. That did not help either and instead caused my jacket to smell worse. I did not care about the look I got when I walked by some people. Luckily for the person next to me on the plane, I put my jacket in the overhead compartment.

I knew a guy I played music with in high school that was living in France at that time and he accepted to host me for a couple of days while I waited for my connecting flight from Paris to New York. I got to Paris and got off the plane with my bunch of stuff, another passenger and I were pulled out of the crowd by French Police officers and escorted to a private room where we were searched and asked to urinate into a cup. Apparently they did an instant drug test on us. As a result of that incident, I started feeling that the stay in France was not going to be a pleasant one. I was so disgusted that I did not even take a shower in France. I could not wait to get to New York. My stay with the Paris friend was uneventful as I watched a lot of TV while my friend was at work all day.

The day I left Paris for New York I called Abena in Cleveland because she was to drive to New York City to meet me before I went to the new summer camp where I was to work. Not realizing how far my Trans-Atlantic flight was going to be I got upset that Abena was still in Cleveland and did not leave for New York yet. I was afraid I would miss her. When she and I spoke over the phone, she confirmed to me that she was just about to leave for New York, and I was relieved.

eibBooks.com
As in Electronic Instant Books
As in eXcellence In Book Selling

Get your book published online instantly, electronically and/or in paperback format like this book and sell it directly on Zongo*Me*.com

We show you how!

PART FOUR

Back in America for Good

CHAPTER ELEVEN

*M*y flight to New York was uneventful and when I got to JFK airport, Abena was not there to meet me. I heard Nelson Mandela was visiting from South Africa and the major streets were blocked for security reasons. It turned out that Abena was stuck in traffic for hours but she eventually made it to the airport where we gave each other a big hug and a long kiss.

We needed to check out of the airport quickly, as I wanted to spend some time with her in New York prior to getting to my new working place summer camp. When we got to Abena's car, I noticed she came to New York with a friend of hers, Shelby and her son Norton. As I got into the car, soon the smell of my stinky shoe-polished leather jacket filled the car and it was obvious we all needed to open our windows. There was a silent agreement between the four of us. So I became conscious of my "cool American style" jacket! We went first to drop Shelby and her son at her boyfriend's house in New Jersey and returned to New York City to the YMCA hotel where I stayed the previous year, but this time Abena was the one that checked in. If I had checked into the hotel myself, my new camp staff that was supposed to pick me up the same day to take me to the camp would have easily located me and taken me to the camp.

I arrived in New York on a Friday and my new camp staff orientation was going to start the following Tuesday. Abena and I stayed all the weekend at the YMCA hotel where we made passionate love. We had breakfast together in a Greek restaurant and I still remember that like it was yesterday. I took a Greyhound bus to Connecticut on Monday and called the camp to come and get me. I was picked up by the camp driver who was from Switzerland. The camp was huge and had a big lake. The camp also owned the land on the other side of the lake. I was assigned a roommate named Mike who was two years younger than I was but was a returning camp counselor at this camp; for that reason he was the lead counselor for our cabin. Our staff orientation was pretty much the same as at my previous camp the year earlier. I guess Abena must have thought something needed to be done in regards to my "cool leather jacket" so she sent me a new jacket to wear at camp. When it was time for the children to start coming, their parents drove in expensive cars to drop them off, and I found out that this new camp was the place where a lot of the rich folks of New England sent their children for camp.

At camp I met an African guy from Senegal, Koussa was his name and he could play very good soccer. We had met briefly the year before when we were on the same plane from Africa. He did not return to Africa the first time he came and got another contract with this camp, which I found out, was open all year. One day while talking with Koussa about camp life, he told me that it gets so cold at the camp that when one urinates outside, the urine freezes before it would hit the ground and I believed him.

At camp there were romantic relationships started left and right between the camp counselors, but I knew I was going to Cleveland to be with Abena so I did not allow any situation to get beyond the level of my camp counselor job. This camp proved to be a lonelier camp for me, as I really did not have anyone to hang out with. Everyone was involved with someone and I did not want to anyone to think I was interested in a romance relationship.

I had the opportunity one weekend to ride with Koussa to the downtown of the nearest small town. Both Koussa and I did not have a car thus Koussa borrowed one from Adam, one of the youngest camp counselors. Adam and I assumed Koussa had a driving license. We got in the car and Koussa drove off the campgrounds and after about five miles, we realized the car would not accelerate pass 20 miles per hour and we were wondering what the issue was. Finally Koussa realized he was not doing something right about this driving thing and asked if I would like to drive. We were on a rural road and I thought since I had driven a car once in Africa I would give it a try. Koussa managed to stop the car, and I got in the driver's seat and drove off. We got to our first traffic light and I pressed the break pedal but could not get any breaking out of the pedal. The pedal went completely to the floor but the car would not stop, so I pumped the break pedal several times with the hope that I would get some friction initiated. I tried to stop the car in vain and before I realized it I was crossing the intersection and running through the red light. Thank God, there was no traffic from the crossing street or we would have been in a terrible accident. Immediately I realized the trouble I was in and decided it was time to stop the car by any means necessary. I drove off the road with the hope that the tall grass would stop the car.

      As the car slowed down I was able to cut off the ignition. We both sat there frozen with all kinds of emotions running through me from anger to gratefulness. We could have been killed at the only traffic light intersection this small town had. I was not sure what Koussa was thinking but he had this grin in his face that made me want to slap him. When I asked him what he thought was going on with the car, he replied he had no idea and neither of us could tell nor needed to know if the other had a driving license or not. We did not even know how to open the hood to go check what was going on in the engine.

      Finally I sat back in the driver seat and examined the dashboard and under the steering wheel trying to gather a clue as to why the brake system on this car was not working. By the grace of God I happen to notice that the emergency brake was in the upward position. This meant Koussa drove the car all the way from the campgrounds with the emergency brake on and the brake pads overheated causing the car not to be able to stop. I lowered the emergency break handle and told Koussa that he was driving the car with the brake on. Then I had the courage to ask him if he had a driving license and he replied NO. Now I understood why neither of us realized that the emergency brake was on. We were both ashamed of ourselves and yet we silently realized Koussa was simply trying to provide us an opportunity to get away from the campgrounds for just a little while. I restarted the car and slowly, still off the road, I now tested the brakes and the car stopped as if it was a new car.

      I made sure I did the test several times before I got on the road. Once I got on the road I tested the brakes several times to make sure. We went to grab something to eat from a restaurant and on our way back to the camp, I would without notice hit the brakes and we both laughed, and that laughter helped us get over the shame we felt over the whole situation. Camp life was uneventful except that finally Koussa slept with Beidy. She was overweight but the nicest girl on the camp. None of the American camp counselors wanted to date Beidy because of her weight. Beidy was happy to finally have the attention of a camp counselor, and in fact the great soccer player. Beidy told the other girls about the experience and very quickly Koussa and Beidy were the talk of the camp. Koussa behaved as if he was ashamed of the talk of having slept with the big girl. I asked if the rumor was true and he confirmed it. As far as I knew Beidy did not hear a word from Koussa till the end of the camping season. Today Koussa is a multi-millionaire soccer player who plays professional soccer in France and plays on his home country's national team at the last World Cup.

    I communicated with Abena via letters and phone calls throughout the camp season and at the end of the camp season, the camp counselors were leaving to go back to their homes. My cabin mate Mike's father came all the way from Ohio to pick him up with their full size van. A few minutes before they departed from the camp, something just hit me, and I asked Mike if they were going close to Cleveland, Ohio. He said yes and that he lived in Akron Ohio which was about 45 minutes drive from Cleveland. I asked him if I could catch a ride and he went to ask his father. His father said no problem. I had 10 minutes to pack my belongings and get on the van. I rushed to the home of Steve and his wife Suzanne who were coordinators of the International camp counselors to see if I could retrieve my visa "pink" form which was essential for my travel across the U.S.

    Unfortunately Suzanne was not in their house and could not be seen anywhere. I started to panic as my ride to Cleveland to be with Abena was waiting. If I missed this opportunity, it could potentially be complex for me to get to Cleveland on my own. Suzanne and Steve did not lock the doors to their home as they lived right on the campground. Instinctively, I went inside still yelling out to call this woman with the hope that she would be somewhere in the house and to my surprise, my very visa "pink" form was laying on the counter in their living room. I simply picked up my form and ran to the van and there we went.

I did not even have the opportunity to say good-bye to the people of the camp. It was past 7:00 p.m. when we left the camp. I was excited and nervous, I finally was going to be reunited with the woman I met one year earlier and had hoped would be my wife. All during the ride to Cleveland, Mike's father would drink coffee and dip his fingers in a cup of fresh water and sprinkle the water in his face. He also listened to a book on tape. At first it really did not hit me why he was sprinkling water on his face until we got deeper into our journey to Ohio, and after having dozed off myself a couple of times I realized he was trying to keep himself awake while driving. I became really nervous and then convinced myself to stay awake as if doing so would prevent Mike's father from falling asleep at the wheel. I was not going to allow that situation prevent me from reuniting with Abena.

The ride to Cleveland took forever as I had forgotten how big the country was. We stopped a couple of times at fast-food stops where we used the restroom and got a snack. When we got close to the outskirts of Cleveland, Mike's father informed me that it would be a good idea that we call Abena to let her know that we were arriving soon. I called Abena from a pay phone and woke her up, as it was 3:00 a.m. I thought she would sound very excited to hear that I was close to her house but I sensed rather that she would have preferred to continue sleeping. I found that a bit odd then, but today in 2004 I truly understand after living here, that after a long day of work, the last thing one wants to do is to be awakened in the middle of the night to meet with anybody.

Abena's house was not very hard to find as she lived off East 105th Street in Cleveland. We pulled into the parking lot in front of her apartment complex and my heart started pumping. I had to face my destiny now; the telegram she sent me in Africa came to my mind, she said in that telegram "I need you to come now and be with me…"

There I was, and as one would say, "Here I am, ready to serve!" The three of us in the van became one team; we were all excited to see Abena and Mike Bass and his father were proud to help connect this love story. I was very grateful for the opportunity the two of them provided me by giving me the ride to Cleveland but I did not know how to express that gratitude to them better than using my words to thank them. I wished I had money to pay them for the ride but I did not have it and I knew Mr. Bass would not have taken it. Right there I learned next lesson about American culture: Most Americans are generous people and would do whatever it takes to lift the human spirit. Abena came out of her apartment wearing her night robe made of an African print fabric and as dark as it was, I could see her beauty shining through the night and straight through my heart. We both ran into each other's arms and had a very long tearful hug. She could not believe I made it to her and neither could I.

She sent for her man all the way from Africa against all odds and there we were in each other's arms again. Mike and his father stood against the van in total silence as both our worlds reunited. It was powerful and they gave Abena and I the needed time to recover from the emotional explosion our eventual physical reunion took us through. I introduced Abena to them and Abena thanked them for having brought me to her, and they said it was a pleasure. Although Mike and I shared the same cabin with 10 kids at the camp, we really were not friends nor had a whole lot in common. The ride to Cleveland was the result of me being at the right place at the right time, and the emotions were so high that before they left the parking lot to go to Akron, none of us thought of exchanging phone numbers.

I really did not know that the way to stay in touch with someone was asking for the person's phone number and I only found that out a couple of days later when Abena asked me if I had their phone number so we could send them a thank you card. She assumed I would have gotten their phone number but I didn't and it would not have dawned on me, as the only way I knew how to stay in touch with a person from my culture was to walk or catch a taxi to the person's place.

eibBooks.com
As in Electronic Instant Books
As in eXcellence In Book Selling

Get your book published online instantly, electronically and/or in paperback format like this book and sell it directly on Zongo*Me*.com

We show you how!

CHAPTER TWELVE

*N*ow I had an address and lived in a comfortable apartment with Abena. Although it was a one-bed room apartment, it was more than any place I have lived in. The place had a nice living room, a TV, a kitchen with a small refrigerator and stove, a bathroom with a bathtub and a flushing toilet. Everything was nice compared to any place I lived in that I could call "my place".

The month of August was nothing but excitement in our lives as Abena and I were so delighted to be with each other. We went to places together and she introduced me to all her acquaintances with pride. I stayed in the house during the day while Abena went to work. I watched TV and did the cleaning of the house. Very soon I realized that I liked American bread, so when Abena went to work I ate the bread. It got to a point that she would come home from work and all the bread would be gone and she could not understand how someone could eat plain bread and keep on eating it till it's all gone! I tried to do our laundry as we did it back in Africa but the only option I had in the house was doing it in the bathtub. I realized very quickly that the laundry detergent sold in America was not meant for hand washing clothes, so I decided to wash the clothes with my feet by sitting on the edge of the bathtub and stepping on the clothes to squeeze the dirt out of them.

After all I had seen people in my mother's village use their feet to peel boiled palm nuts to make palm oil so I figured what could be worst than that. But Abena found that to be the funniest thing in the world, the way I was doing the laundry. I timed it correctly so she did not think I was just sitting in the house doing nothing. She came home and found me in the bathroom doing the laundry with my feet. She didn't say hello or anything she just started laughing, laughing and laughing and more laughing, to the point she was in tears, and I could not understand what was so funny about me doing the laundry with my feet! I was simply trying to take care of business you know. As the bread eating continued, Abena realized that we were going to have to do something about that. She got mad at me because this time she just got a loaf of bread the day before and the whole thing was gone by the end of the following day. She said to me, "we are going to need to find you a job". I had no idea how to find a job nor what kind of job I should seek. The following weekend, she bought the Sunday newspaper and looked through it to find me a job. We found a couple of job listings where the requirements were "no experience necessary". I did not know that one was supposed to wear a suit and tie to a job interview.

Abena had recently graduated from college and came to Cleveland to help a friend coordinate a summer cultural festival. She stayed in Cleveland afterward and now she was the program manager of a non-profit organization Ohio, Inc., which provided arts, sports and tutoring programs for poor children in the inner city. She took me to the basement of her work building where they kept donated clothes and shoes for distribution to the poor people in the housing projects. She had me try on a couple of suits and the best that fit was a brown suit with white pinstripes with a modest bell-bottom pair of pants. We found a nice tie from the stack but the challenge was how to put the tie on.

My father never wore a tie so I had no idea how to put one on, but I could not let Abena know that, the male pride somehow snuck up on me on that one. We got home and I had the whole weekend to practice putting on the tie since the interview was on Monday morning. Believe it or not putting on a tie without any instruction can be emotionally dangerous for the novice. It took me hour upon hour of trying to put on the tie without looking like a goof ball, but I eventually figured it out, all on my own, and this success was one of the achievements I am proud of. I felt so proud and smart and confident that I knew I could do anything. Monday Morning came and I had to get up early to to go catch the bus to get to the interview place. Abena gave me a leather planner to carry in my hand so that I would look really professional; she even made me get a fresh hair cut for the occasion. I first thought she was kind of pushing the haircut thing a bit too far because I only cut my hair by myself once a year in Africa and could not see what a big deal it was to have a haircut prior to a job interview. But I must say that with a fresh haircut and my suit and tie, I looked sharp!

I got to the interview place where a whole lot of people had come for the same interview as me. They had us sitting in a conference room like we were in a doctor's office and would be called one at a time to see "the man". After waiting there for about 30 minutes, two young men came to the room with nice suit on and greeted us with big smiles on their faces. One of them took the lead and did all the talking while the other one kind of stood by him and had some catalogues stacked up next to him.

One of the gentleman introduced their company as an International Marketing company for fragrances, and due to their rapid expansion, they were in need of sales staff to cover their Northeast Ohio market. Everything sounded really good so far and I started to get excited, as I know I could sell anything because, when I was a young boy, my mother would make donuts that I would go to sell at the marketplace. I would have a glass box with the donuts in it and walk around the market yelling out to catch the customers' attention with things like "Call me the donut selling young man" and the women in the market would indeed call me to buy my donuts. I did pretty well and my mother was so proud of me.

So I thought I could sell anything, the thought of selling perfumes did not sound too bad at all, and after all, I needed to do something and could not continue eating up all the bread as I quickly understood from the home-front. The "mass interview" continued and it became clear that before we became sales representatives for this company we were going to have to sign a contract through which we were going to purchase our first kit of perfumes for selling door to door. I left out of that interview a bit depressed, as I felt even if I wanted that job, I could not have gotten it because I did not have money to buy my sale's rep starter kit. I also realized that I could not be successful in that business, as I did not know a whole lot of people that I could go sell perfume to. I could tell that Abena was proud of me even though nothing came out of this "interview". It was good that I was out of the house with the hope of finding a job. We realized that I would need a driving license in order to eventually get a car to drive to work where ever that work might be and also as a form of identification. In order to get the driver's license, one needs to have a social security number. I went to the social security office and was told I needed to prove that I was authorized to work in the US. I told them that I came to work on a summer camp as a camp counselor and they said they needed to see a pay stub from the summer camp. I showed them the pay stub of the $250.00 the summer camp paid me for my work. Luckily for me I still had that pay stub at that moment. I was issued a social security number.

Abena still had her station wagon that she nicknamed the green machine, which had a stick shift transmission. The night before I start practicing driving the green machine to prepare for my driving license test, we were going to visit a friend of Abena's and drove through a neighborhood in Cleveland and the green machine was shot at on the windshield. She continued driving this time faster as we knew something was up. As we got to the friend's house all shaken by the incident, I rubbed my finger on the cracked windshield spot and smelled gunpowder. Our friends thought it could not be a real gunshot but rather a bb shot; nevertheless, I was shaken.

Meanwhile I got another interview at an agency where they needed a classroom aide in a school setting for emotionally disturbed children. I once again put on my wonderful brown suit and went to the interview. It went very well I thought and a week later I got a job as an Associate Teacher Counselor (ATC). With that job I was to be a certified teacher's assistant in a classroom of 10 children with emotional problems. The salary was $15,000/year and I was excited and felt I had the chance to truly get into the American system. During the interview, the interviewer told me that he was convinced, considering my resume and educational background that I could do the job but for my own sake I ought to go to an American university and get a bachelor's degree for job security in America. When I left Africa, the government statistics indicated that the average person in Togo earned $350.00/year and there I was with a job that would pay me $15,000/year, I said to myself I love America.

    I caught the bus to get to my new job every day. About one week after I started on the job, the principal asked me if I would be interested in driving some parents to the school using the school van for parent-teacher conferences in two weeks time. I responded yes that I would, knowing that I did not even have a driver's license. I was not going to allow a simple thing like driving prevent me from integrating into this system. So when I got home that day, I told Abena that I really needed to get a driver's license because I had been offered the opportunity to be parents' driver for overtime pay. Abena went to the license bureau and got me the driving rules book. I knew I only needed to get the theory part right for the practical part of driving, I had seen enough people drive coupled with my first time driving in Africa that I would be okay. I studied very hard on the driving codes and when we went to the driving test, I passed it the first time. It was like the doors started to open in front of me; I did not have to carry my passport as a form of ID.

    Things started going very well now between Abena and me for now I had a job and we could buy more bread if we needed to! September ended and we realized that my visa was expiring at the end of October 1990. I knew the ATC job with the emotionally disturbed children could not help me with my visa situation. The alternative was to find me another camp counseling job with the YMCA camp system that I thought at the time had the authority of requesting an extension to my visa or getting married. In my mind getting married was the ultimate choice because I was in love with Abena. I came to find out that Abena felt the same way too but unfortunately for me I did not know that the man was supposed to ask the woman to marry him. In Togo, the man's sisters or aunts would be the ones responsible for going to the bride-to-be's family to ask for her hand for their son, the groom.

    So despite the burning desire in me to want to marry her, I was remembering what I went through in Africa with Amelia who told me that the only reason I wanted to be with her was for the opportunity to come to America. I truly did not want to have to go through that scenario again and traumatize myself with that issue. As time was running out I realized that I had nothing to lose and one evening before we kissed good night we were both laying on the bed after a long discussion on my immigration status, I gathered all my strength and asked her if she would marry me! She said, "Finally! What were you waiting for?" Then I realized that she really wanted to marry me but was simply waiting for me to ask her.

Abena got excited and picked up the phone to call her mother who was living in Silver Spring, Maryland. When Abena's mother heard the news, she was delighted, and told Abena that we should come to Maryland to get married and that she would take care of everything. I had no idea what getting married in America meant and simply followed Abena's lead on the matter. We picked the date of October 20$^{th.}$ We decided to get a rental car to drive to Maryland, as the green machine would not be a car to use for the "just married people". It was a nightmare trying to rent a car to go to the wedding because neither one of us had a credit card. We finally wrote a post-dated check to one of Abena's friends and asked her to rent the car for us. We ended up getting a two-door sedan because that was the only one we could afford.

The wedding was scheduled for a Saturday and we left Cleveland on Thursday evening for Maryland. We drove during the night and got to Maryland where we stayed at my future aunt-in law's house. It was the first time I was meeting my mother-in-law to be and her two sisters, and it was the first time I was spending the night at her sister's house. I was nervous but thought to myself, I had to be a man and be on top of things.

Knowing that I was not going to know anyone participating in the wedding, I sent out an invitation letter to an ex-girlfriend of a Togolese buddy of mine who lived in Washington D.C. To my surprise this lady came to the wedding with her husband who was also Togolese. At least there were two people I could speak Togolese to at my wedding. I was very nervous as more and more people showed up all dressed up in

African garments. I smiled a lot and carried myself the best way I knew as a gentleman. My brother-in law who I met the day before was assigned to be my best man, whatever that meant. Everybody was beautiful, even my father-in law who the rest of my family-in law has not seen in 10 years flew in from California to give his daughter's hand to me.

    My father in-law is a Vietnam veteran who unfortunately did not recover as one would hope from the wartime trauma. That contributed in my opinion to the difficulties experienced by this beautiful family I was marrying into. Despite all that was said about the man, I give it to him for doing whatever it took him to fly in all the way from California to give his oldest daughter's hand away despite the potential that he could have been prevented from attending the wedding altogether. True love transcends every challenge we have in life I would say on that. Abena had on a beautiful wedding dress we had ordered custom made for her in Cleveland, but she and her friends just could not figure out the hair-wrapping thing and they were laughing at themselves silly in her dressing room. I was out in the main living room of Abena's aunt's house where the wedding was being held, and I was a nervous wreck. Before I left Togo, my father gave me a gold lace fabric outfit that he told me he received in payment for building a house for a wealthy man while he was in the financial asylum in the country of Benin. He gave me that outfit as something valuable of his that he had hoped I could sell in America and use the money for food. Well, that outfit came in handy for my wedding as it fit right into the occasion. At first sight, I look like a real prince from Africa; I looked very rich and proud.

    My mother-in law and her sisters took care of every arrangement for the wedding. A Methodist minister conducted the ceremony. I was very embarrassed to kiss the bride in front of all these people because showing intimate affection publicly is something one just did not do in my culture, so I gathered my strength, closed my eyes and I KISSED the bride and it felt good. I was officially married to the woman I thought was a dream away. Abena's old theatre group sang to us, and I was very moved by their acappella singing. Abena and I wrote a song titled "On the Other Side of Sunshine" that we performed at the wedding, I played the guitar and Abena sang a duet with me. Afterwards, we were served a wonderful dinner, opened the wedding gifts and then had the wedding cake. I heard that the new groom and bride are supposed to feed each other cake and smear it on each other. Abena and I took turns feeding each other, but passed on the smearing part. We danced and talked with her friends and relatives until it got late in the evening.

My mother-in law made a reservation for us to spend our wedding night in a classy hotel in Silver Spring but when we got to the hotel, we were too tired and fell asleep until the next day. I learned later that on the wedding night, I was supposed to have made passionate love to my new wife, but we both were too tired and fell asleep as soon as we got in the hotel room.

We got back to Ohio and I resumed my job with the emotionally handicap students. We bought an old Datsun hatchback for $500.00 from a colleague for me to drive to work. It was driving my car home from work that I experience my first snowfall. I drove very fast home because I wanted to be able to feel it, touch it and smell it before it all went away I thought. I got home, parked the car, ran into the apartment, and took off my shirt and shoes so to truly feel this snow thing with my body and feet. I ran back outside and started to dance in the snow with bare feet celebrating my first snow. The only snow-like thing I had seen in my life was the frozen ice in the freezer in people's refrigerators that I came across in Africa. Wait a minute, this snow thing was getting too cold on my feet, so cold, I had to run back very fast into the apartment and put my feet over the heated radiator. Abena was laughing at the whole thing she could not help herself.

The next day as I was going back to work in my two week old used car I realized that I burned out the engine because I was driving the car without enough engine oil in it. There went my hard earned $500.00. Now we needed to get me another car to continue going to work with. On a Saturday Abena and I went to a car dealer to look at cars that we could possibly buy.

The car dealer told me he could help me get a car but because I did not have any credit history what so ever, I would need to bring a co-signer for the car loan. I had $500.00 cash on me as down payment and the dealer took the money and told me I would need to bring in my co-signer on Monday for the car loan paper work. At least he would let me take the car off his lot because I told him my job location was far and I needed a car.

Since Abena was fairly new in the town the only person with good credit she could think of was an 83-year-old lady that she had been introduced to and was helping write her memoirs. The following Monday, I took all the necessary information from our 83 year old co-signer to the dealer because the old lady was not feeling too well. When I presented the information to the dealer to start the paperwork for the car loan, he burst into laughter when he saw the birthday of my co-signer. He thought we were trying to pull a joke on him, and he got angry with us. I told him sincerely that I was new in town all the way from Africa and the old lady was the only one with good credit I could find. The car I was trying to buy was selling for $1,600.00, which with financing would have cost me $2,400.00.

The car dealer rejected my co-signer's information and the only option I had was to pay cash for the car or go somewhere else. I was getting angry and thought of the American system as unfair as why couldn't the dealer trust me on my own word that I would pay the monthly car note? I thought why would he think that anyone would buy a car from him and refuse to pay the car note anyway? Why wouldn't he give me a chance? Out of anger and disappointment, I asked him to give me back my $500.00 deposit I had given him on the previous Friday as down payment.

Due to the fact that he did not have the $500.00 cash to return to me on the spot, he was stuck and now asked me if I would be interested in taking a look at one of the other cars he had on the lot. My first choice was a red two door Ford Mustang that I drove all weekend and loved but now I had to go with a four door Dodge Caravel. At that point, any car was all that mattered to me. He finally did the paperwork without using my co-signer information. I had to pay $150.00/month until the car was paid for. That was how I got started building up my credit history in America. If it were not for the fact that the dealer did not have my cash on hand to give me, I would have missed the opportunity to start building a credit history.

Everything was good, work was going well, except the children with whom I was working would call me names like "African butt naked" and tell me "why don't you go back to Africa to go feed your people?" At times it became necessary to physically restrain them to prevent them from hurting other students or themselves, and in the process, they would spit in my face and call me all kinds of names. These kinds of behavior were unthinkable to me as respect for authority was something your parents and our whole society "banged" in your head growing up so you wouldn't even dare talk back to your teacher or any adult. I remember when I was in school and there was a behavior problem, the school principal invited the child's parents to the school and the child in question was whooped, in front of the whole school. There I was being verbally "abused" by these children and no one did anything about it except give them a low rating of "1" on the behavior modification sheet on scale of 1 to 3. I accepted soon enough that it was part of the job that I had and that these kids were testing me to see if I was just like the other grown ups in their lives that reacted so predictably to their negative behavior.

Now that I had a car to drive, I learned soon that I needed car insurance. It became clear that my $15.000.00/year job was not enough. I got a second job as a group home attendant part time. I also decided to place flyers around to find people to whom I could teach French. The first person that responded to my ad was a man who left us a voice mail message. When Abena listened to the message, she sensed something weird about the message. She told me that I ought to meet the person in a public place and that she would go to the meeting with me.

We needed the money but something just did not sound right to her about this response to my French teaching ad. I called the guy and setup an appointment to meet in the public library so we could discuss how I would teach him French. Abena and I got to the library on time. The man came and we both were able to identify each other by the way we described ourselves over the telephone. He was a short Caucasian man wearing a yellow rain coat over his shirt. We greeted and decided to go find a quieter place in the library to talk. There was a book and craft fair at the library so Abena went to peruse the crafts and books. I went to the basement section with this man and we sat at the table. I pulled out my notebook in order to take notes about subjects that were of interest to him so I cold target my lessons to satisfy his needs. He said that he'd always wanted to learn French and that his family owned a fishing equipment store so he would be able to pay me well if I chose to teach him French. So far so good, then I asked him how long he intended to take my classes. He said he wanted to have lessons on a long term basis and then, he said, "French just turns me on". For a second, I did not know what he meant, and then he moved his chair closer to mine and put his hand on top of mine. I felt uncomfortable and then I got the meaning of the "French just turns me on" thing. I removed my hand quickly and told him that unfortunately, I needed to leave at that moment. I told him that I wanted to teach real French to people. I felt like punching him in the face but I did not. I quickly walked out of the library basement and I was furious. Abena was right about the message the guy left on the answering machine.

Abena was glad she told me to meet in a public place. I did not give up; I placed an ad in the local newspaper and got a tutoring job for two children whose parents worked in France and wanted their children to continue learning French. So at times I had three jobs, one full time one and two part time ones.

December came and I experienced Christmas the American way. Abena and I put up a small Christmas tree and exchanged gifts on Christmas day. It was very special. The custodian of our apartment building lived next door to us. At midnight on December 31st the custodian went on his back porch and started shooting in the air but I did not know it was he and who would be shooting so close to our bedroom I wondered. I had a flashback and did not know what was going on. Abena was so calm on the bed and I wondered why she wasn't worried. Out of panic, I jumped off the bed and attempted to get under the bed but we did not have a bed frame to go under.

Our mattress was directly on the floor so as the guy continued to shoot in the air, I could not help it but try to go under the mattress. I made it under the mattress and now the mattress was lump-sided with my new wife pinned between the wall and the lower side of the mattress. To my surprise Abena found my reaction to the gunshots to be so hilarious she could not stop laughing. I thought she ought to be dead-quiet at that moment because her laughter would have signaled the "perpetrator" that we were indeed inside the house.

I stayed under the mattress until the guy stopped shooting in the air. When I got out from under the mattress all dusty, Abena could not look at me without breaking into laughter. I had to explain to her what I had been exposed to in Africa and I could not help but panic when I heard gunshots. She hugged me and then explained that in America, on New Year's Eve, some people like to shoot in the air to celebrate the arrival of the New Year. I wished I knew that because I had just made a fool out of myself in front of my wife who I was supposed to protect. I actually had hoped that she followed my lead and came under the mattress with me but she did not. I thought, I guess she is American thus free to allow herself to get killed, as she did not follow my lead to get under the mattress.

In February, I received a letter from my sister in Africa and as I was reading this letter, it said, "Please go find a chair to sit down". I went to sit down, and as I continued reading the letter, my sister was informing me that my mother had died two months earlier. She said that they took care of everything and they simply did not want to cause me unnecessary suffering considering they knew I was struggling here in America and would not have had the means to go to the funeral.

I was devastated at the thought of not being able to give my mother a dollar from my salary before she died. I was also saddened to think that she would never meet my wife and that I would not see her again.

When I went to work the following Monday, I told the principal of the school about my loss and he told me that had he known of my mother's death earlier, he would have collected money to help me fly back home to Togo. That meant a lot to me to hear that from the school principal. At times I felt guilty wondering if my mother died because she was heartbroken that her only son left and was not coming back, and at times I had to convince myself that I have a life to live and I need to continue making decisions for myself.

Since I had a job in America now, I decided it was time to start making payments on the money Suzie from Switzerland gave me to help me with my plane ticket to America. I called her up and told her that I was ready to start making payments and she told me not to worry about it and that the next time I went to Africa to make sure I bought a bicycle for a girl and one for a boy. I could not believe what she said and I was blown away. She was my angel. If she did not come into my life, I would have missed the opportunity to come to America. I told my wife about it and we both were very thankful at her gesture.

Time passed and Thanksgiving came and I was feeling so blessed and fortunate that I decided to call up Suzie to once again tell her thank you. But this time when she picked up the phone, she told me she did not want to hear from me again. I was shocked and asked her what was going on? She told me that the whole African experience was a fiasco for her and she went on to explain that she had gotten pregnant all because she went to Africa. Oops, did she say that? But I figured it could not have been me, as she would have told me the last time I spoke with her in February or so.

She continued to tell me that before she met me in Nigeria, she had met a gentleman from Finland who was doing some work in Cameroon, the country east of Nigeria. When that gentleman was on his way back to Finland, he stopped by Suzie's place in Switzerland and they had a one-night stand and she got pregnant. The man did not want to have anything to do with the pregnancy, and Suzie did not want to have an abortion. So she was all "messed up" at that time, then I called. So she decided she did not want to be reminded of Africa at that point thus she told me never to call her again!

Abena decided to also interview for a position at the same agency and got a job as an Associate Teacher Counselor as well. She also decided to go back to school and got a master's degree in education. We moved to a house on the west side of Cleveland near the west side market. We joined an African dance company that was started by some of Abena's friends. She and I played drums for the company, sang and did storytelling as well. We also started to make African jewelry and clothing to make extra money.

After 3 years we decided to have a baby, we figured that people who were poorer than us had children and survived. We felt we had a lot to offer a child. Abena stopped taking her birth control pills and we tried. Abena got pregnant after our first try and nine and a half months later we had a beautiful daughter. We named her Afeewa because she was born on a Friday. I am grateful that my mother-in-law and my sister-in-law were able to come to stay with us to help us with the baby. In Togo, the man went to work and the woman would take taxi to the hospital to deliver the baby and she would take taxi back to the house then the man got involved. I was proud of myself for being able to witness the birth of my daughter. No, I did not pass out!

During this time I also applied for citizenship. I had to study and pass a test on American history and the constitution. I am glad to say that I passed the exam and was proud to be part of the group of immigrants that pledged my commitment to the United States of America. It was an emotional ceremony, as the land of the FREE was officially becoming my land and I thanked God for all the wonderful things that were happening to me in my new home. We had a son in 1998 that I named Lodonou.

As Lodonou got older, he wanted to go ice-skating like her sister. Imagine the only snow –like thing I ever seen was the frost in the freezer section of a refrigerator. Here I was with my son who was six trying to teach him how to ice skate. I held his hand and we slowly got on the ice. That's it I would say to him trying to muster up the slight display of confidence I've seen in him so he does not loose his temper due to both our inability to ice skate properly. Then we fell, and we fell and he fell. I tried to make the falling part a learning opportunity by saying things like, "that was a good fall".

      The third time we went ice-skating there was a woman and her daughter skating against the wall. She was attempting to walk as if she was on the cement floor. As I was telling my son that one should not attempt to walk on the ice as if one were on the ground, I needed that woman to confirm to me what I was telling my son was the correct thing. To the contrary and to my surprise, the woman said yes that it was the way she was taught 20 years earlier, but hearing me talk to my son she thought I was some sort of ice skating expert that had the new and improved skating techniques. At that point I said to my son "I really don't know". At that very moment that I said I didn't know to my son, I was reminded that I am an African. I really did not know how to teach my son how to ice skate. We managed to take a break and on our way home I mentioned to my wife that we needed to see if we could enroll the children in ice skating classes. That same day Abena enrolled both children in a skating class. What a relief!

eibBooks.com
As in Electronic Instant Books
As in eXcellence In Book Selling

Get your book published online instantly, electronically and/or in paperback format like this book and sell it directly on Zongo*Me*.com

We show you how!

Starting My Business in America

CHAPTER THIRTEEN

I remembered when I interviewed for my associate teacher counselor job that I was told to attend an American university to secure a bachelor's degree. So as my new family settled in, we decided I should attend college in America. I decided to major in International Marketing because I realized the potential of my language skills and figured if I completed my degree I would be able to find a better job quickly. I decided to attend a local university in the Cleveland area. After I registered for college, all of a sudden, I received VISA and American Express credit card application forms in the mail. I filled them out and I had credit cards.

The college I chose was close enough that I could go to school in the evenings. I inquired about financial aid and had the opportunity to get student loans. At first I did not know that when they meant financial aid, it was loans that were to be paid back. This was different than the financial assistance in Togo where the government gave students financial assistance that the students did not have to pay back. The only stipulation was that the student had to keep good grades.

My first trip back to Africa was paid for with student loans (should not have done that). If I knew what I know now, I would not have gotten so many student loans. Despite having student loan debt, at least I had the opportunity to pursue my education here in America. I graduated with a Bachelor Degree in International Marketing in 1995. I was especially proud to march with the graduating class during the commencement ceremony. I felt like I, the son of my mother had earned a degree from an American university despite the fact that my professors in Africa thought I was not smart. I wished I had come to America earlier in my life so that I could have experienced college years without having to work, being married and trying to understand the American culture all at the same time. Student life in Africa was not exciting at all. We were afraid to trust each other as students because of the fear that your peers might turn you in to the government and you would be gone without trace. We had this fear on the campus that the government had infiltrated the student body with spies and it was just not enjoyable. Discussions on politics were totally out of the question. When I came to America, people could call the president of the United States all sort of names, tell jokes about him and no one go to jail. I was amazed.

About six months after graduating from college, I went on the Internet and ran a search for French speaking jobs in Ohio and found a company that was looking for a person who spoke French, to train and support their French speaking Canadian customers. I applied for the job and was called in for an interview. During the interview I found out that the salary this company would start me at was more than I expected and that to make the same amount of money at my then current Associate Teacher Counselor job would have taken me 15 years.

The choice was clear, I decided I needed to move on and accepted the job. Since I was going to be taken care of the company's Canadian customers, they decided to send me to Canada for the first two weeks for field training. I was to go hang out with one of their French senior salesman to get myself familiar with the business and to acquaint myself with the Quebec accent. I flew in to Canada and at the airport I realized that I did not have my passport with me. I had been delayed at the airport waiting to be able to get in touch with my wife so she could fax me the copy of my passport for proof of identity. Meanwhile the salesman that was supposed to pick me up at the airport was getting desperate and wondering what had happened to Tino. When I finally got out after a 45-minute delay, I walked up to the man with the sign showing my name on it and called his name. I could tell that he was shocked to see me and I could not figure out why. He was expecting an Italian to come off the plane because my name was Tino he later told me. I believe I do a good job at this company but unfortunately; some people just could not handle a smart black man.

Certain people at my workplace could not believe that I could speak four languages fluently. Unfortunately for the company I would say, even management could not recognize value in their employees when there was one. I witnessed favoritism, and I hate to want to put it this way, institutional racism. I don't know how else to explain it. There was another black guy who worked in the same department as me and he was hired one year prior to me. After I was hired, they hired two Hispanic women. One had a Bachelor degree in early childhood development, the other a bachelor degree in English. Two years later these two women had been promoted to higher positions with higher pay than both of us two black men.

During my training to learn about the various product lines, I was sent to a training class in Connecticut. At that training class there was a white gentleman who came from one of our distributors stores to learn about our products just like I did. One year later this gentleman was hired to join the department where I worked. Two years later this gentleman was promoted to a higher position. This gentleman told me that he did not even finished high school but now is a Product Manager. Obviously he was being paid a higher salary than me, a black college graduate.

Meanwhile the other black guy and I somehow had been pushed to the side and given the title of technical writers without having gone through any training in technical writing. Obviously, I can do anything, and in fact I have been doing technical writing for the last five years. The problem I saw was that I applied for numerous internal job postings but the response I got was basically, "you just do not have direct experience". Imagine a Technical writer for an American corporation who learned English watching TV. At one time it was reported to me that one of the managers said, "Why does this Tino always bid for jobs, is he trying to sue us?" As they drive expensive cars and live in big houses in the suburbs, they could not understand why a person like me would want to better my family's position in this life by wanting to get a better paying job that would provide me with higher income, especially when I know I am qualified for those jobs. I wanted to provide a better opportunity for my children so when they grow up they would not have the hard time I had starting up. One of my ex colleagues had been promoted to management position and he had an associate degree in theology and worked with me in the same department for three years and knew all about my African origins. But after the September 11th attack on America, I met him in the men's room and we started small talk and to my surprise this guy asked me if I ever traveled to Afghanistan. I was so devastated at the fact that this guy had the nerve to even ask me that question. After I left him, I got angry at myself for not being quick enough to respond to him and say "Yes I have been to Afghanistan with your mother".

    A couple of days later, the global brand manager was talking to the ladies working in the cubicles next to me and this manager said, "I probably will get reprimanded for this but Tino are you a Moslem?" I responded, I was not Moslem but I am an American citizen. If corporate America in general is run like this company, America is in for big problems because we cannot continue to expect to continue making money "by default" or as in "cruise control mode" just because of our company name. It got to the point where I came up with solutions to real problems that would save the company huge amounts of money but they would not listen to me and would rather go spend thousands of dollars to pay a so-called third party company to come up with the same solution I just shared with them.

    I told management time and time again that because I had worked at learning information technology on my own, I had a different perspective on understanding issues related to software and customer interface coupled with my International Marketing degree. But they won't listen to me because in their minds, I am just the technical writer guy from Africa. It got to the point where I did not care any longer. I just watch them waste money that we could have saved as a company if only they would listen to me. I felt like I was trapped in my position, I was too qualified for my job and yet they would not give me the opportunity to move into a better, more challenging and more paying position. I have written to the HR department, to the global marketing director to let them know of all the skills that I have acquired throughout the years that could really help our company. Management's attitude to me was like I should be happy I even have a job. I pointed out to them in a conference call with the Marketing Director for North America, the Global Marketing Director and the HR Director that I needed them to be aware of my skills and that were not being utilized to the fullest. I explained that since I did not seem to be qualified for any position within the North American operations I would be interested in our International operation should a position become available that required language skills like mine. I reminded them that I had an International Marketing degree and could speak fluently French and Spanish.

The HR director's response was, "You understand that you will have to do more work on top of your current workload to prove that you are capable of the things you would like to do". I told them that they should bring it on. I knew well that my ex colleagues that were promoted to bigger and better things, were not asked to do more to show that they were capable of doing their new jobs, they were simply given the opportunity to excel and if they did not have the skills, the company sent them to training all over the place to learn the skills close to where the job requirement were. It became clear to me that this company was not interested in equal opportunity as far as my employment was concerned. I got more motivated to start my own business and apply my brilliance to my own thing. With the experience in corporate America, I strongly believe that "true freedom" is in the entrepreneurial spirit in America. It does not come easy but if you work hard at it, America allows you to be rewarded handsomely.

Meanwhile the younger brother of my childhood friend Eddy needed me to help him find a market in America for African garments that he would export to the United States. Due to the fact that I had a full time job and could not physically help him, I thought maybe if I had a web site that would be a central marketplace for sellers and buyers come to do business I could help him better that way. I went to speak to computer service people and they told me that all I needed was a computer to act as a server and the Microsoft FrontPage web development program.

I ordered the server and the necessary programs Everything was delivered to me and I asked how was all that supposed to work, and I was told that I could either pay them $75.00/hour to do the work for me or I could get the books at the bookstore and figure out what to do on my own. It became clear to me quickly that I just spent $7000.00 on computer equipment, and software and I have not even start my business yet. The choice was clear to me. I did not have the financial means to pay anyone $75.00/hour to get the web site setup for me. So I went to the book store to buy the books I was told to buy. I purchased a Microsoft Windows NT server administration book and a book on how to use Microsoft FrontPage. I stayed up late at night studying and trying my best to learn web site development in order to accomplish my goal.

There was no going back since I could not return the hardware and software I just purchased. Besides my wife would not let me live in peace if I just left all this hardware to collect dust. I needed to create a database driven web site so that the sellers could register their company or business information and the buyers would be able to search the database and find the items or services they were looking for and be able to contact that seller for business.

The challenge that I faced with the web site model was not for the novice that I was. I found myself calling the Microsoft help desk late at night because I could not do it during the day. The people there were fantastic, and I could understand why Microsoft became such a successful corporation. Their technical support had an A+ rating in my book. They did not shuffle me around through a labyrinth of departments. I was hungry for knowledge, and those people helped me pickup the fundamentals of database search coding that I needed to get started. I am very grateful and I hope this book sells enough copies so I can contribute financially to the Bill Gates Fund to educate people on information technology.

My first web site was up and running in 1998 but I used too much color on the site because I thought it needed to be pretty. The prettiness did not do me any good as I came to learn that not all computers display color the same way. When I viewed my web site from a public library computer, it really looked ugly and I was crushed. The first domain name I registered for my site was www.GlobalMarketSales.com. I needed the name of the web site to say it all. So the name of my company is Global Market Sales Co., U.S.A. Ltd. I chose to add U.S.A. at the end of my company name because, lets face it, despite all the negative publicity, America is still the country with whom most of the world still wants to do business. So I figured the U.S.A. in my company name would give the company the grandeur, the credibility, the pride I wanted to convey. I like to think big, and my head was getting "bigger" as I began to see the potential for entrepreneurs in America.

I registered my company with the Secretary of my State so that I could do my taxes as a DBA (doing business as). I lived on Martin Luther King Drive, and I had to go rent a mailbox to use as the mailing address of the business. The reason was that I was told that if I use the Martin Luther King Drive address for the business, automatically people would know that my business was a black owned business and there is a segment of the population who would rather not do business with a black company.

Since I wanted the company to be a global market sales company, I did not want to cancel out a certain segment of my potential customers. It has nothing to do with being proud to be a black business. Because I needed my company to be given a fair chance, I rented a mailbox in Shaker Heights, which is a city known for its affluent residents. So when you hear of Global Market Sales Co., U.S.A. and the address is in Shaker Heights, it puts people at ease, I could tell by the look on their faces.

One reality though was the fact that I have an accent, despite my effort to sound like an American. My African first name doesn't help me neither as when I say my first name which is Kodjo, immediately people would say oh Koo-jo, and they know I am from Africa. But if I say my name is Tino Adognravi, then they think I am an Italian. Although I am very proud of my African background, I like the intrigue Tino Adognravi produces in people. As I was going through the difficulties of developing my web sites, I remembered that you should never put all your eggs in one basket. I decided that because I could not get my web site up soon enough, I should start making African clothes myself. I just believe I can do anything if I apply myself to it. My father told me that only my intelligence would take me far.

I bought a used industrial embroidery machine for $1,600.00 but found out that the machine ran too fast for my skills thus I could not control the speed and the free hand artwork this machine could produce. With the use of a pulley system I was able to create a distributed speed for this machine. I could then really go slow and be able to produce stunning African design embroidery. I thought I could make African hats which if I sold 100 a week at $10.00 each I would be okay. I was in the basement of our first house doing embroidery listening to the best of Rush Limbaugh on radio and heard an interview of Congressman Jesse Watts that was so moving to me that I was then convinced I was on the right track. I would not give up and I would do whatever it took to make it in America. There I was on a day off from my full time job, instead of watching TV, I was working trying to better my life and provide a better future for my children.

I invested in software and domain name registrations to the point that I was in so much debt that I needed to get credit counseling. I had to get into the credit-counseling program not because I went and spent money frivolously but rather spent money on my business.

One major mistake my wife and I made was that our first house was the best house on the block and when it came time to sell the house to move, we could not sell the house for the amount of money we owed on the house. We needed to pay off a $17,000.00 home equity loan we had on the house to be able to sell the house. The home equity loan was also used to purchase my computers and software for the business. Luckily we had a husband and wife who were (and still are) our friends to whom we explained our situation about the sale of our house. This couple decided to get a home equity loan on their house in order to lend me the $17,000.00 so we could close on the sale of our house. I only gave him my word that I would pay them every month until the $17,000.00 was paid off. I call them our very good friends and I am grateful for them.

In other words, do not get in so much debt in order to make your house the best house in the neighborhood unless you plan on retiring in that house.

In an attempt to create multiple stream of income, I finally came up with the following web sites:
- ZongoMe.com same as Globalmarketsales.com and LooksiteMall.com
- Consult4me.com A directory of all consultants worldwide
- eibBooks.com eXcellence in Book Selling.
- BeatBalls.com (you may listen to and buy the beat balls there.
- UltraJobs.com (Jobs and resume directory worldwide)
- BestClassroom.com (Worldwide directory of training courses etc.)
- MilleniaPhone.com (Online meeting with crystal clear audio using a headset)
- PhotosPlace.com (A worldwide marketplace for photos)
- http://www.KwanzAmall.com
- http://www.LebronJamesFans.com
- http://www.Looksite.com
- http://www.UltraRomance.com
- http://www.MissKwanzaa.com
- http://www.BestSportsMall.com
- http://www.GeoCamping.com
- http://www.AllPerformers.com
- http://www.AllTranslations.com
- http://www.RoboCalendar.com same as RoboEvents.com
- http://www.RoboTickets.com
- http://www.SalesCoupons.com same as IwillBuyToday.com, AllNationsCoupons.com, AllSalescoupons.com

I also came up with a way to share my wealth with anyone willing to take advantage of my six years of hard work. Basically anyone who is interested in making money off the Internet could signup to become an Affiliate of Global Market Sales Co. U.S.A. Ltd. Once you signup, our complete web site is automatically duplicated for you with your name on it as in

Zongome.com/Yourname. You may, during the signup process choose to have additional homepages for your web site that will be generated for you.

This means that you could choose to have your web site address be PhotosPlace.com/Yourname or RoboTickets.com/Yourname. How the affiliate makes money is as follows: Once you get your own web site address, for example www.ZongoMe.com/Tino, the word Tino above would be replaced by your own name or the username you entered during registration, you would make flyers and business cards with your own web site address (URL) on it. You pass out the flyers or your business card to as many people as possible. Basically the web site generated for you becomes your business. The more people that log onto your site and sell items or use the MilleniaPhone from your site the more money you will earn in commission. The commission table can be viewed on either of the web sites above by clicking on the "Become our Affiliate" link. Once a user comes to signup through your web site, anytime that user sells something or signs up to use the MilleniaPhone online telephone with crystal clear audio quality, you get a commission when they pay Global Market Sales Co., U.S.A. Ltd for using our services. You get a percentage of the fees the sellers pay for selling the items on our sites. You do not have to worry about customer service as I have taken care of that aspect already.

All you do is promote your own site. Please do not send unsolicited e-mail to people. If you do and we are notified, your account will be simply deleted without notice. We believe that you do not need to send spam e-mail to others in order to take advantage of our system. I have done the hard work for you and all you have to do is promote your site. You may put an ad in your local newspaper, get some lettering signs for your web site address and stick it on your car as I did when I first started; it's effective. People will see it and it will be on their mind when they sit at their computer. With your imagination, the possibilities are limitless. Every third Saturday of the month, from 2:00 to 3:00 p.m., I have a teleconference from our site using the Millenia-Phone and you are welcome to join in to listen and ask me questions. I have done the work and now I am successful but I would like to make you successful as well, because if you become successful, you will be able to help someone else become successful.

You have read my story now and saw how people helped me without expecting anything in return. So I want to help others with the hope that they help others and the ripple effect continues to lift the human spirit on this earth. Who would have believed that I would be writing these lines with the confidence I have and the belief that anything is possible and that people would actually spend money to read my story? When you can think of it, it can happen. It's all about how bad you want it to happen. If you are hungry for it, please join my team of International Affiliates of Global Market Sales Co., U.S.A. Ltd., you will be glad you did. One other thing, which in itself is not a must but rather a hope of mine is that once you sign up to become an affiliate of Global Market Sales Co., U.S.A., I am inviting the affiliates to voluntarily become an "Angel" for a child. Simply pick a boy or a girl to whom you would pledge to give words of encouragement to so that child can achieve all his or her potential. This child could be your own child or someone else's. I will personally meet with you online via MilleniaPhone meeting facility to hear your success stories.

Maybe together we could put out another book of our success stories about your efforts to empower the selected child. My father did not give me money but he told me that only my intelligence would take me far and here I am in America and founder of a potentially multi-billion dollar Corporation. Global Market Sales Co., U.S.A. Ltd. Publisher of the Global Market Sales Family Web sites with the common portal at www.ZongoMe.com.

Since you have purchased this book, you may submit your request to be entered into our drawing for 25 people to accompany me to Togo for the film shooting of the documentary about what you read in this book. Please submit your interest to president@globalmarketsales.com to let me know in which area you could possibly assist with the project.

In the subject line of your email please enter Coming To America film project. I am looking for people who have experience in the following areas: (Please Note that you do not have to be an expert in these areas to be in the drawing. If you are one of the 25 winners and you do not have any of these skills, we still would love for you to join us on the trip). We will pay for your trip and lodging while in Africa.) Note: we will only do the drawing after the first 1,000,000 (One million) copies of the book are sold. So please tell your friends to buy the book so we can reach the drawing level.

Area of Interest for the Coming to America Project

- Video camera operator, Video technician, editor
- Photographer
- Writer/screen play writer
- Lighting specialist
- Makeup artist
- Audio recording specialist
- Would learn or help with anything specialist
- Investors
- Sponsors

Send your email of interest to:
president@globalmarketsales.com with the subject line: Coming to America project.

eibBooks.com
As in Electronic Instant Books
As in eXcellence In Book Selling

Get your book published online instantly, electronically and/or in paperback format like this book and sell it directly on Zongo*Me*.com

We show you how!

CHAPTER FOURTEEN

I needed to go back to Togo because my father was getting older and I knew he had testicular hernia that was getting worst at this point in his age. I wanted to help my father but I did not have enough money in the past years to be able to help him. I had tried in the past to buy him a hernia belt that he could wear but the type that I found in America was not strong enough to help him. In January of 2004, I convinced myself that I needed to go back to Togo for fear that the next news I would hear from my family would be that my father has passed away.

Not knowing how I was going to get there, I finally thought of my retirement savings from the company I worked for full time. I decided to borrow against part of my retirement savings to go to Togo. I bought my plane ticket and was scheduled to leave on March 24, 2004. I could not give the specifics of my arrival date to my people in Africa for fear of too many expectations on me that I could not financially afford. So I called my sister who works at the hospital in the capital city to let her know that if things went well, I would be visiting at the end of March but was not sure.

About a month before my departure, I made a flyer that I posted at my workplace requesting that my colleagues donate their old summer clothes that I could take with me to give away to people in Africa. I collected a lot of clothes and shoes from my colleagues and was able to fill two heavy-duty duffel bags and a large suitcase. The day before my departure, I called the travel agent to confirm whether security at the airport would go into my bags as I heard from one of my colleagues that bags and suitcases are no longer being locked during travel. The travel agent told me that I should not worry and that in fact I was set to check my luggage one time at the airport from my departing city and I would get my luggage once in Togo I was to fly from Cleveland to Laguardia airport in New York then from JFK to Senegal and Senegal to Togo. I got to the Airport in the morning with my three giant pieces of luggage and carry on bags. I learned at the airline-checking desk that I was misled by the travel agent and that flying to LaGuardia and from JFK was a two-city process. I was also told that my first flight carrier would not transfer my luggage between the two airports, and because I had an extra over the limit luggage, I had to pay an $85.00 charge. I figured $85.00 for the ability to donate all the beautiful clothes my colleagues gave me was not a big deal. I got to LaGuardia Airport at about 10:30 a.m. and had to take the bus to JFK airport. I waited for about 25 minutes and a silver bus came and I was the only customer to climb on board. The bus driver was a Caribbean guy with a lot of gray hair like me. Since I was the only passenger on the bus, I sat in the front passenger seat and started up a conversation with him. We talked about the recent deposition of Haiti's President Aristide and just had an honest man-to-man conversation about politics.

We got closer to JFK airport and as a sign of appreciation for the good conversation we had, I thought I would give him a $5.00 tip. I pulled out my wallet to get the money out and left the wallet on my lap. When he stopped the bus for me to get out he stood up and said "After you sir" so I stood up gave him the $5.00 not knowing that I had just dropped my wallet. I proceeded to get off the bus and he followed me down to the luggage compartment where he helped me collect my three heavy pieces of luggage. I thanked him for the ride and we both were pleased to have met each other.

Now reality hit me, as now I had to find a way to carry all my overloaded bags and suitcases around the airport until 5:00 p.m. for my next flight. I got one of those airport heavy-duty carts that I managed to set everything on. It was very difficult to maneuver this cart, as it was simply heavy. I made it through the security checkpoint and slowly made my way to the food court, used the washroom and decided to eat lunch. Since nobody was supposed to leave his or her luggage unattended, I once again slowly managed my cart to the restaurant storefront to place my order. I reached for my wallet and it was not in my pocket. Panic time! Where could my wallet be? Then I immediately recalled that the last time I took it out of my pocket was on the bus from Laguardia airport to JFK airport to give the bus-driver a $5.00 tip.

The Way It Was *Coming To America:* The Real Story.

Unfortunately the buss had no identification I could only recall that I the bus was a silver bus. I rushed to the airport security people to relay my situation to them and they said they could not do anything except to call the Airport Police for me. Meanwhile I had been told to go upstairs to the Taxicab dispatcher's desk to get them to page the bus for me. How in the world was I supposed to make it upstairs with my luggage since I could not even ask anyone to watch it for me? I was getting very angry and worried about my credit cards inside my wallet.

Luckily I had my traveler's checks, passport and plane ticket in my kangaroo-pouch that I had on my waist. I barely made it inside the elevator to go upstairs. I got to the supposed Taxicab dispatcher's desk and when I explain the situation to the attendant, she said, I would have to get out of the building and walk around to go find the bus dispatcher for help. How was I supposed to leave the building, walk across the street and around the building to find this person to help me? I felt I would have kicked the travel agent in the groin if he showed up at the moment.

Slowly but surely, I made it to the area indicated to me and found out that the station I was sent to do not handle the busses. The attendant gave me a flyer with a New York phone number on it and advised me to give them a call to see if they could radio the my bus driver from me. Well, I had to get back into the building to make that call from the pay phone. Sweating and upset, I managed to get back inside the airport after having to go through the security checkpoint once more! I had $250.00 cash in the wallet and all of my credit cards, the picture of my wife and children and an Ohio lottery ticket.

I called the number on the flyer and they were able to reach the bus that I took to JFK but the bus driver said he did not see any wallet. So my wallet was gone for real! Now that I got back inside the airport, the airport police came and I explained the situation to them and they told me the best thing they could offer me was the form to fill out a Police report. I filled out the form and they gave me a copy for my records. I managed to call my credit card companies via the 800-information hot line and all of my credit cards were cancelled. It was time to check in for the flight across the Atlantic Ocean. As I walked up to the airline ticket desk I asked to speak to the manager as I knew I had extra luggage but I had only planned on paying once for the extra luggage in Cleveland as I was told by the travel agent. They got me the manager and I explained my situation to him and asked if there was any provision in their policy for an exceptional case where the manager could make a decision to assist the customer. He told me there was no provision and that I could pay the $350.00 for the extra luggage or throw the luggage away and that he did not write the policy.

If I had my credit card, I would have been able to put the charges on my credit card. The whole situation was like a nightmare. Eventually I had the courage to speak to a Senegalese traveler who agreed to lend me the $350.00 cash and I would pay him back once on the other side of the ocean. Twenty minutes before departure time, I realized that I did not cancel my gasoline credit card and I panicked. If I did not cancel that card, the person who might have my wallet would have been able to charge gasoline in my name.

I called the gasoline credit card customer service agent and was on the phone trying to repeat the spelling of my last name for the millionth time. Eventually the customer service agent located my account and taking her old time trying to read whatever was on my account. I was called to board the plane and the only thing I could say to the customer service rep was "I lost my wallet and please cancel it". We boarded this Boeing 747 jumbo jet. As I sat down on the plane, I had to convince myself to remain calm and optimistic and to believe that the loss of the wallet was just a part of the risk of traveling. I had a whole isle to myself and was able to write part of this book on the plane, as I did not have to worry about any neighbor that my laptop screen would disturb. The flight over the Atlantic Ocean was uneventful.

The plane was so big that the turbulence could only be felt slightly. We landed in Senegal early in the morning around 7:00 a.m. My connecting flight from Dakar Senegal was scheduled for 11:00 a.m. thus I had three hours to kill at the airport. I wanted to take the opportunity to visit the famous Goré Island but with the experience I had in New York, any attempt at any type of adventure was out of the question. We went to the duty free shop at the airport in Dakar where I was able to get some CFA (West African French Speaking Countries' currency) to pay back the Senegalese guy who helped me in New York City.

In Dakar, all the passengers' luggage was brought to the main lobby and I was not going to loose track of my luggage so I sat at a distance where I could, at all times monitor my luggage. I found myself sitting about five feet from a gentleman who was skinny and smoking a cigarette. Noticing that he was smoking alerted me that I was in a different country at that time. Upon first sight of that gentleman, you would think he was just one of the grounds cleaning crew. I stroke up a conversation with this gentleman and found out that he was a businessman from Guinea on his way home from a business trip to China.

We had a great conversation and he illustrated to me how Dubai was becoming the import/export center of the world because of their "tax" structure. Diallo was his name and we hung out inside the airport, had lunch together and talked about everything from politics to culture. He told me that he became a businessman because of a Togolese woman, who mentored him in Guinea. He was happy to meet another Togolese person this time coming from America. 11:00 came and we took off from Senegal with a stop in Bamako, the capital city of Mali.

The plane landed in Lome, the capital city of Togo around 7:00 PM. As I stepped off the plane onto my native land, it was dark, everything appeared so quiet and calm as if all the trees and flowers knew I was coming. As I mentioned earlier, I told my sisters that I would be coming at the end of March with no specific date. I followed the line to customs I was hit with the reality that I was returning to Togo as an American. The custom officer requested my passport, I handed him my passport and was told that I needed to pay for a visa, which was going to cost me $15.00. I had lost all my U.S. dollars in New York and did not think of getting extra cash while exchanging money to pay my Good Samaritan in Dakar.

I panicked because the custom office was not set up to accept travelers checks and it was so hot that I could not see myself wasting more time in "another" airport. I knew my buddy Tsphore would be at the airport to pick me up. So I told the custom officer to allow me to walk to the glass wall to signal to my friend that I needed some money. I prayed that he would have that amount of money on him.

I could not see my friend in the crowd that was standing against the glass wall, but there was a gentleman that I thought I recognized who smiled at me and signaled that he would meet me when I got out. What a relief to know that someone was there to pick me up. So I signaled back to him that I needed $15.00 for my visa and hoped that he understood me. He came to the door and introduced himself to me and informed me that my friend Tsphore was tied up in a meeting and had sent him over to pick me up. I told him that I needed $15.00 to pay for my visa and he reached in his pocket, pulled out a wad of money and gave me the equivalent of what I needed to pay for my visa. The custom officer told me that he was giving me a temporary visa and I was to get to the main office the following week to get a long term visa.

I was happy to see that my entire luggage made it safe to Togo and all I had to do was pass through customs and I would be home free. All went on smoothly and off we went from the airport. Gerald, the guy who came to pick me up brought a minivan and a helper. Somehow they thought I was coming back with my whole family. I had to tell them that I could not afford to bring the whole family to Togo at that point. Gerald and the helper informed me that Tsphore was expecting my family and me. Once again I realized that I was in a different country because I was sitting in the front passenger seat of the minivan and could not locate a seatbelt to put on. Gerald was driving too fast on a road where the streetlights were not what I am used to. I convinced myself that it would not be a long trip since my buddy only lived 15 minutes from the airport the last time I visited in 1997. We did not go to his house as I was expecting, instead they took me to downtown to one of my buddy's stores where they needed to pick up few things to take to his home. Then I remembered that my buddy had moved about a year ago to a new house he built near the beach. When the minivan arrived at the house, the garage door was opened immediately by the night guard who heard the car coming. I was impressed because the house was large enough that he needed someone constantly in the house as a security guard.

The heat was getting to me as no matter what I did, it was simply too humid. I was setup in the downstairs living quarters of the house. He had hired a chef to cook for us for the entire 14-day stay. We went upstairs on the veranda, which was open, and we could feel the breeze from the ocean coming through. As we sat on the veranda, Tsphore told me he had been out of the country the previous week on a business trip to Dubai. He said he made arrangements for the mechanic to get his other car ready for me to use during my stay, and that we were going to visit the mechanic the next day to see if the car was ready.

The first night was hot despite the electrical fan and I had to sleep naked and still was sweating. I called my wife and children to inform them that I made it safely despite my problems in New York. The next morning Tsphore and I drove in his new Mercedes Benz, which I found, did not have a working seatbelt. I was not too concerned about that because we were going to the mechanic to see if my own car was ready, and I hoped it would have a functioning seatbelt. The head mechanic was not there but the car that was supposed to be fixed up for me appeared to have been in this shop for the last 5 years with everything you could think of missing from the car; from the engine to rear-view mirror. The message given to us was that the part needed for the car was more expensive than the amount of money Tsphore gave them prior to his trip to Dubai. So instead of buying the part and fixing the car and charging Tsphore the difference, they did nothing and waited for him to get back in town so they could inform him of the additional expense.

As I looked at that car, I told myself that there was no way those people could fix the car before I went back to the U.S. Somehow, Tsphore was still convinced that they would be able to fix the car for me if only they had the right part. Unfortunately, the only place the part could be bought was in Cotonou, the capital city of the Republic of Benin, the country east of Togo. Tsphore said we were going to Benin the next day to get the part and that it would only take 2½ hours. The car was a Mercedes station wagon. Prior to my arrival I told Tsphore that I would like to rent a car from Avis and he told me I need not worry about it and that he would arrange for me to have a car when I got there. We went to his office in the commercial center of the capital. I took his Mercedes to go visit my family and came to pick him up later and got back to the house for lunch.

As I drove to the market of Bè, I stayed in the car and asked a passer-by to go tell my sister that "her brother was back" from America and was waiting in the car over there. I did not want to just show up for fear of causing her to have a heart attack. The last time I went unannounced to Togo, I was talking with my older sister in her room and my father came by to discuss a construction project with my sister. When he saw me he simply fell backward and passed out. I had to take his shirt off and fan him and pinch his cheeks to revive him.

This was my younger sister Sidonie who came to the car all excited. When we saw each other we embraced in long hug and we were both crying from the joy of seeing each other again. After the hug was finished, she took the fabric she was holding in her hand and started to hit me with it as if saying, "You crazy brother! How could you do this to us? Couldn't you even let us know the date you were coming?" My younger sister Sidonie owned her own store where she sold beauty products. I was proud of her. I sat in the store and we sent for my youngest sister Marceline. When she came we gave each other a long hug and cried together. I was very happy to see them again. We talked and talked and talked. It started getting late and I needed to go back to pickup Tsphore but I could not do so without having gone to my older sister Genevieve's house. My sister Genevieve was like our second mother when we were growing up. She did everything for us and I stayed with her to finish high school. I got to Genevieve's house, parked the car and walked to the house. The gate was open and facing the gate was Genevieve sitting in an armchair taking a nap. I thought quickly that the last thing I wanted to do was wake this woman up and the first thing seen was her brother that was supposed to be in America. So I went back to the car and saw her neighbor who I explained the situation to and asked her to go wake up my sister, tell her that her brother was back from America and was waiting out side in the car.

    Genevieve rushed out of her house to come to see me; we gave each other a long hug and both cried tears of joy. We talked and talked and I told her I needed to return the car to Tsphore. They were disappointed to here that I came in the night before and was not staying with them. I told them that I hope they would understand. When my friend Tsphore came to the US, he stayed with me and I prefer staying with him because he had running water and a flushing toilet, which are kind of nice. Besides, the first time I returned to Africa, I left my luggage at my sister's house and her son and God knows who else went into my things and stole stuff from me. It was difficult asking my family who took what, and to avoid any further situations; I decided to stay at Tsphore's.

    The next day Tsphore had to stop by his office to take care of some business before we hit the road for Cotonou to go buy the right part for the car. We left the city around 11:00 a.m. and as we got on the highway, I realized that the Mercedes did not have functioning speedometer. I had to wrap the passenger side seatbelt around myself and to feel as if I had some sort of protection in that car. Tsphore must have been driving over eighty miles per hour and I was mad and frustrated. I told him he needed to slow down and he laughed at me and called me an American scarecrow. I could not let go of the thought of returning to Africa and getting killed in a car accident the next day because of failure to wear a simple seatbelt. I was furious but felt helpless, as this well-to-do African guy could not understand when I said that my insurance would not cover me if we were in an accident and I did not have a seatbelt on. Besides, I did not want to get hurt. He laughed and I could not wait to get back to Lome.

The Way It Was *Coming To America:* The Real Story.

When we hit the border between Togo and Benin and I had to go through the customs with my American Passport. I had to pay for a visa to visit Benin and had to kindly explain the reason someone had come all the way from America the night before and had to travel to the next country the following day. As we went through customs and got back onto the road, we saw this beautiful lady that Tsphore greeted and offered ride to. She accepted and got in the car and off we went. She was from the town right after the border. We had to get off the main road and go close to the ocean to drop her off. Tsphore promised her we would stop by on our way back to Togo later that day.

I really could not enjoy the ride to Cotonou because of the speed issue. I saw on the side of the street under the hot sun, people selling gasoline in giant glass bottles setup on tables on the side of the street. I could only imagine the danger of that but should one need to get gas, you stop by one of those tables and the lady would come out of the woods and measure the gasoline for your car. The unfortunate thing about buying gasoline from the side of the road like that was that you do not really know what you were putting into your car. I heard people would cut the gasoline with kerosene in order to make extra profit. As we got closer to Cotonou, Tsphore informed me that he needed to make a detour to go deliver some wine to one of his customers. It was hot and his car did not have any air conditioning. We went to the customer's house, she was not there and he decided we could wait a bit as they said the lady should be there soon.

All along, I was concerned about the way back to Togo as I noticed the night before that the headlight beams on the Mercedes were not aligned properly. One could not see the ground just ahead of the car. The passing car drivers thought that you were flashing them and they would flash back at you to signal you to lower the beams of your headlights. I knew there was no way to lower these headlight beams before we got back to Lome and that was the least of Tsphore's concerns.

Finally, we got to the Akpakpa market, one of the largest marketplaces in the region. We had to walk through a maze of kiosks to get to the parts vendor. This parts vendor was about 22 years old and vending auto parts was what he did for living. He would go to the next country of Nigeria to buy the parts and bring them to Benin to sell in a sort of "black market". I was just amazed with the way these young men knew the parts name and where they go on a car. They did not have a computer system, everything was from memory and a small notebook he had in the drawer of his small classroom-type desk. As Tsphore was trying to negotiate the price of the new part we needed, the young man pulled out a copy of an old receipt he gave Tsphore two months earlier clipped together with the money he received for payment. I asked him why he wouldn't take his money to the bank knowing that the marketplace could catch fire any time and he would loose everything. His response was that his money was safer at the marketplace than anywhere else, even at the bank. We've got the part we thought we needed and took off for Lomé.

Now Tsphore wanted to go see his brother who is a translator. He wanted to introduce him to me because I mentioned to him that I had developed a web site with a URL www.Alltranslations.com. Of course when you go visit someone, it is the custom that the host offers the guest something to drink like a soda or nice cold water. We got to his brother's house and sat in his small store adjacent to house where I had to explain to him the business concept behind the www. Alltranslations.com. He sent someone to go buy us some soda. We drank the soda and talked for a bit and then headed off. To my surprise, Tsphore said he needed to stop by his sister's office to get some fish to take to Lomé. We stopped by the sister's office. His sister's office was half air-conditioned and we were in the air-conditioned section where the sister worked and food was ordered for us to eat.

Since Tsphore sisters did not know we were coming, no one had ordered the fish and now that we showed up, the sister sent for the fish. It was about 3:00 in the afternoon. I was growing frustrated but had to convince myself that I had 14 days and it was only the second day in Africa. Hopefully we had the right part and the car would be fixed for me in two days or so. Tsphore decided that it was important for me to go see the "door of no return" where the slaves were sent off on boats destined for the

The Way It Was *Coming To America:* The Real Story.

Americas. As we were driving toward the ocean, there were statues of the various kings that reigned during that period of time and the symbols representing their reign. I really did not care for these statues at that particular moment, as I was more concerned about our ride back to Lome. We passed two young Caucasian ladies that were walking in the opposite direction and were probably just coming from the door of no return. I took a couple of pictures of the door of non-return and on our way back. We slowed down the car and I could tell by the way the Caucasian ladies dressed that they were American. I spoke English to offer them a lift should they want one. They were shocked that in the middle of nowhere, they had just found someone from the United States. They declined the offer and we continued on.

I thought the nightfall would encourage Tsphore to want to get home as soon as possible but to my surprise he decided to stop by to see the lady we picked up earlier at the border. As we got to the house, it appeared that the lady took us to someone else's house and pretended that was her house. She forgot to figure out in advance where the light switches were in the house she took us to. She mistakenly asked someone where the light switch was. Tsphore and I looked at each other and knew it was time to go very soon, and that we were dealing with a game player. The remainder of the drive home was as stressful as in the morning, I could tell that Tsphore was tired but somehow he thought because I was from America, I could not handle driving at night in Africa. I thought to myself, if only he knew how driving in America was he would have trusted me and let me drive. It got so bad, that he eventually asked me to drive. As soon as I started to drive, he fell sound asleep. We got to the border and went through customs without any incident. We got home around midnight and the chef was still waiting for us to get home and to serve us dinner! I was very happy to be back in Lomé safe and sound. I prayed that we had the right part for the car so I would not have to endure that emotional torture I felt in regards to the seatbelt issue and no speedometer on the car that Tsphore drove me in.

The next day, I went to see my father very early in the

morning. I needed to get there early enough so that I did not miss him. My sisters told me that my father had moved onto the land that I purchased in Togo for $2,000.00. My father built two bedrooms on the land and he and my stepmother had moved there. When I parked the Mercedes, my father and my stepmother knew it had to be me as they were told a day earlier that I was back. They ran to come to greet My stepmother cooked Akoumey and gumbo sauce that I reckoned she was the best at. My stepbrothers and sisters and my father and stepmother all ate the akoumey from the same bowl and it felt wonderful to be able to eat together with them. We talked for a long time and I found myself being the master child-rearing specialist as I watched my step sisters interact with their children. I could not help it but to give them advice about positive reinforcement for their children.

It was interesting to see my father speak to us, he apologized to his children for the fact that he was not able to provide us with the best opportunity we could have had; but the fact was that he wished us good health and best wishes. We all cried and I gave them the gifts I brought for them. Besides the summer clothes that I collected from my colleagues of work, I had purchased a solar powered, hand crank radio with a flashlight and lamp, which I showed my father how to use. Since they had no electricity in the house, this was a treasure.

I needed to take the car back to Tsphore and had to cut my visit with my father short at 11:00 a.m. My father told me that he would visit me the next day at Tsphore's house. The car situation was just not making my stay as smooth as I would have liked it to be. I had to wait for Tsphore to be done with his errands before I could use the car.

My father came the following morning to visit me. He had taken the scooter taxi and got to the place around 7:30 a.m. while I was still sleeping. The night guard woke me up and I went to see my father whom surprisingly looked older than the day before. I later found out that he had an earlier hernia crisis that morning. My father had a testicular hernia for as long as I can remember. When I was a kid, I remember my father would wear a leather belt around his private parts to prevent his intestines from falling down into his scrotum. With time my father could not find replacement for his hernia belts and had to improvise.

That morning when my father came to visit me we started talking and he invited me to the nearby room and said he needed to show me something. My father started unbuttoning his pants and I realized soon enough that he was going to show me his hernia. When I saw my father's genitals tied up with a rope and his testicles as big as a grapefruit, I told him, "Dad we are going to the doctor tomorrow". I never saw anything like that in my life and I was ashamed that my father had to live with anything like that.

I went and called Tsphore so he could have a peek at my father's hernia so he would know the severity of the situation. I needed to pickup my father around 4:00 a.m. so that we could get to the hospital in Afagna early enough to be seen first by the doctor. Afagna is my mother's village and the hospital was built there by Franciscans brothers from Italy and somehow was believed to be the best place to go for the best health care. I had hoped that I would take my father in and get him in the surgery room right away but found out that we needed to have some preliminary blood tests and x-rays done first. The surgery itself was to be scheduled for the following week. As my father and I waited in the crowd to get the ticket to go see the consulting doctor, one of the nurses started an AIDS awareness education program with the crowd. I was so proud to see that there was an initiative to educate the masses about AIDS.

The wait to pay for the preliminary test was getting long because people would not follow the rule of first come first served. I eventually was able to get the ticket to see the doctor. We were directed to go sit in front of an office removed from the crowd. The male nurse that was preparing the doctor's office for our visit walked by and I thought he looked like one of my cousins I grew up with. I asked him if his last name was Sallah like my mother's. He said yes and we talked about his brothers and sisters. The nurse said he was the operating room nurse and that he would be assisting the doctor when it was time for my father's surgery. Surprisingly, the doctor looked familiar to me but I could not remember where I knew him. After he examined my father's condition, he asked my father how long he had the hernia problem; my father replied since 1964. Both the doctor and I were surprised to hear that and the doctor asked him "and you lived with this for that long?" My father affirmed this and said that he never had the money or the courage to go through with the surgery.

The doctor had hoped we could get the blood work done that day but I had just gotten my father some donuts to eat prior to us getting called in for the consultation. I had to think quickly and remembered that my elder sister Genevieve was a lab technician and could help us with the blood work. The doctor said as long as the lab was a reputable lab it did not matter where we had the blood work done. We decided to get the X-ray taken care of in Afagna and walked to the building designed for that. The area was crowded. We got in line and it was very hot. The designer of that building did not at all in my opinion take into consideration the ventilation of the building.

As everyone just sat there without any knowledge of what was to be expected or what we were supposed to do in that hot hallway, I poked my head into the x-ray room and surprised two guys simply chatting in their air-conditioned room. One of them abruptly stood up and came to the door as if to say how dare you open the door without being invited. He kind of chastised me indirectly. So I came back and sat next to my father. A few minutes later, a 10-year-old girl was wheeled out of the x-ray room with full body cast on. I asked what happened to her, and her crying mother said she was hit by a car that fled the scene. Car insurance was not something I was aware of while I lived in Togo.

As I was growing impatient and concerned about being able to return the car back to the capital city for Tsphore to use, I decided I needed to talk to someone to make sure I was at the right place to begin with. At times I felt very sorry for these indigenous people who could not read and did not have someone like me to come to the hospital with them. There were not logical signs to follow and if it was stressful for me, I could only imagine what it would be for those farmers that had to be there that morning. So I walked up to this nurse in a white nurse robe and waited for her to finish talking to someone. She was done talking and as I said hello, and started politely to address her she hand signaled me to stop talking and said "you are the husband of...." I said no, not me, and she eventually said, "you are the brother of Da Valerie" and I said YES indeed, and at that particular moment I could see in her face the traits of my mother's lineage. She had three vertical ethnic identification scars on each of her cheeks.

So I said to her "you are the daughter of uncle Mensah" she said yes and her name was Caroline she added. She told me that she was the nurse who attended my older stepsister when she came in for a colonoscopy and later died. We gave each other a polite hug and she told me that she was the sister of the male surgery room nurse I saw earlier.

I explained to her our reason for being at the hospital and she told me I would not have to worry about a thing. She would take good care of my father when the time for the surgery came. She took the paperwork for the x-ray from me and went in and a few minutes later my father was called in to have his x-ray taken. I was happy to be able to find my cousins at the hospital and relieved at the fact that even if I was not going to be in Africa for the surgery, some family members would be able to look after my father. We did every thing that need to be done that day and before we left the hospital, my cousin Caroline said she needed to introduce my father and me to someone.

My cousin escorted us to the next building and right before we entered this room, she said in a quiet voice that the person we were going to meet was our cousin. He was a doctor and that the doctor's late father and my late mother were close cousins. When she opened the door, it was the surgeon who examined my father earlier that morning. Caroline introduced my father and me and we were all so amazed at how small the world we live in is and how everything kind of went in a circle for us that day. I was pleased and relieved and my father was confident. My father said he was ready for the surgery and that he was tired of suffering. Before we left my newly found cousins, I asked the doctor permission to allow me do give them some money as family members, not as doctors and nurses, for taking care of my father. He took it and we all laughed. I gave them the equivalent of $50.00 I needed to pay for the surgery in advance in order to secure the surgery schedule. All in all with medicine, time at the hospital after the removal of the two testicular hernias, the procedure cost around $500.00.

    My father and I got back to Lomé around 4:00 p.m. I dropped him off at his house and gave my stepmother some money to go shopping for food supplies for the house. I needed to go see my sister Genevieve early enough so that she could follow up with the blood test arrangement. My sister took a look at the paperwork and said she would have to go to work despite being on vacation to help with the task at hand. My father had to wake up early to catch the scooter taxi to Genevieve's house and together they would go to the general hospital in the capital city where she worked. The actual surgery was schedule in two weeks, which meant that I would be gone by then. I was disappointed that I could not be there but I was happy that I was able to help setup the surgery for my father. After all, he was my father and the man, despite not being able to provide me with material wealth or money, seized the opportunity at times to empower me as I mentioned earlier.

    There were a couple of people that I wanted to be able to see this time while I was in Africa. I had hoped that the second car for me would have been fixed by then, but somehow the part that we bought in the Republic of Benin was the wrong one. So I had to juggle the car with Tsphore until the beginning of the last week of my stay when I got a car from Edu the son of Mrs. Lastima of Chicago. See, when I went to visit Mrs. Lastima in Chicago before my trip to Africa, she had given me pictures for her son in Togo. I made an appointment to meet with Edu to give him the copy of his mother's certificate of naturalization and to visit him as well. After explaining to him my predicament with the car, he decided to help me out. He was traveling out the country and decided to allow me to drive his Ford Taurus. Now I had mobility and could take care of my business without worrying about having to return the car to Tsphore.

    I looked for Didier and his family so I could thank them for having taken me in for a whole school year without any financial help from my parents. Didier's father decided to allow me to live with them because of my friendship with Didier, which allowed me to be closer to the high school we went to.

    I left Lome at 5:00 a.m. and hoped that I got to the city of Aneho early enough so I could possibly catch the people I needed to see before they left for their daily activities. Aneho is at about 65 miles from the capital city and I relied on my memory to help me locate the house where I lived together with Didier and his family. I kind of knew there was a slim chance of Didier's family still living in in that house because they were renters, but I needed to take a chance at that point. These people had helped me but I was not able to say thank you to them, so I was on the mission to achieve that. At the old house, there was a man to whom I explained my mission and as I was describing Didier's family, his wife thought they might have a picture of Didier's older sister. She went into her room to get the picture. She returned and to my surprise it was in fact Didier' sister in the picture and her children. The man said he could help me find the family who now lived in Lomé where I had just come from. We got in the car and returned to Lome to go find Didier's sister. I found them and when they saw me, the three sisters ran to me to give me a hug as if I was their true brother. We hugged for a long time and we all cried tears of joy. I always loved them, but just was never able to express that to them and show them my gratitude for them having me in their lives for an entire school year. We talked briefly and they informed me that their father has died two years earlier following a diabetes induced limb imputation. We planned to go actually meet Didier later that day uptown. I gave money to the man who helped me find them so he could take the public transportation back to Aneho to his family.

    I went to see my own sisters and then went to meet with Didier's sisters. We went to see their mother and together we visited Didier my high school buddy. Due to time constraints, I could not spend much time with Didier. Didier was now the educational program director for a private high school in the capital city. I had to meet with Didier in his office because he had to work and that was the only chance I had to meet with him. We talked about our respective families and life in general. As I told Didier that I wanted to see him again to show him my gratitude for what his family had done for me, he told me that he reached a point in time when he just blanked me out of his mind. Hearing that from him truly hurt me, for I always thought of him and his family and due to my personal circumstances I simply could not find them nor could afford anything to thank them with. In any case, I did what I could at this time by sincerely thanking him and giving him, his sisters and mother some money.

I decided I needed to see my first high school girlfriend to apologize to her. You may be wondering why anyone would want to apologize to a girlfriend after 25 years. Well, when I was in the 10th grade, I was naïve, stupid and un-mentored thus while I was "dating" this girl and I did not know what I was doing. I think we must have had un-protected sex two or three times. I realized that my then girlfriend stopped visiting me and I was not able to find her and no one could tell me where she was. Apparently, I learned six months or so later that she had gotten pregnant supposedly by me. Her older sister with whom she was staying took her out of town to the capital city where she was forced to have abortion. When they came back to the town we were living in she was forbidden to see me. I vaguely knew where her family lived in Lome but was not so sure as to where. I decided I needed to close that chapter of my life by finding this woman and presenting her with my apologies for her pain and suffering.

Once again my memory did not fail me and I was able to locate her family's house. I asked about her and they told me that a young lady could escort me to where she lived. I was nervous and did not know what to expect. As a security precaution, I wore shorts and flip-flop sandals so I would not attract attention to myself as being from America all throughout my stay in Africa. I had my passport and money wrapped in a plastic bag in a waist pouch inside my pants. A would be pickpocket would have to work extra hard to steal my money. As the young girl and I entered the compound where my ex-girlfriend lived, a man came to the window to look at us and signaled to us to come upstairs. I thought that was my ex-girlfriend's father. I got upstairs and when this now woman came out of the room, at first she could not tell who I was. Then I took off my baseball hat and she said, "Who is this, who is this, who is this" in disbelief. We both started crying and at this time I could not say if they were tears of joy or if they were tears of lost love that never had the chance to bloom. I thought the man was her father thus out of respect I did not give her a hug or anything. She introduced me to the man and told me that he was her husband.

Upon hearing that, I was glad I did not give her any hug with all that crying. I introduced myself again to the man and told him his wife and I were friends long time ago. I told him that I now lived in America and had a family there and that I was coming to his house humbly and in peace. I told him that due to immaturity, I had created a situation that might have hurt his wife a great deal thus I was on the quest to seek her forgiveness. I lowered myself in a sign of respect in Togolese manner and asked his permission to ask his wife for forgiveness. He gave me the nodding go ahead. So in words, I asked Ayele to please forgive me for the pain and suffering my immaturity might have caused her throughout the years.

While she was still crying, she asked me "so you came all the way from America to ask me to forgive you?" I said yes, and she said, "I forgive you Valentin". She said Valentin in the same way she used to call me, which she knew I knew was her special way to call my name. At that point although she was crying, I knew that by saying my name that way, she was communicating to me that she was happy inside. My tears also were flowing. I said thank you to her and thanked the husband for allowing me the opportunity to ask for forgiveness.

I decided to give her some money so she could buy breakfast for her children as the custom suggests, then I realized that I did not take out my money prior to entering the house, thus still have my money all wrapped up in a plastic bag inside my short. I asked where was the bathroom as if the bathroom would be on the same floor as in America so I could go take the money out in private. Realizing that there would not be any bathroom anywhere, I simply walked away from them, faced the wall, unzipped my short and started taking out the money. I wanted to give her some money so badly that I did not realize that any money taken out of the groin area in front of any husband would not be welcomed. The intensity of the moment did not allow me to think clearly of the potential consequences of any misperception of me pulling money literally from my underwear to give someone's wife. As a sign of respect I tended the money to the husband with the wish that it is used to buy breakfast for the children, he directed me to hand the money to Ayele. (Which husband would have taken the money retrieved from another man's groin area!)

    She took the money and thanked me. I told them that I was going back to America in three days and that I was very happy to see her again and appreciated her forgiveness. Both she and her husband escorted me back to the door and I got in the Mercedes and left. As I got in the car and left it just hit me that I might have created a situation that could potentially lead to marital problems for that couple. Then I prayed and left it in God's hands, with the hope that the man continues to see the whole situation with serenity as he did all throughout that episode which lasted for about 10 minutes. The lady did not know I was coming and she has not seen me 25 years I would say. I pray that both of them and their children find some peace and that my visit did not cause any disturbances in their relation. At this point there is no way for me to find out as any remote attempt to find out could potentially initiate what I would hope did not happen at the first place. My friend Edu who let me drive his car while he went to Burkina Faso was supposed to come back to town so we could discuss his mother. We wanted to talk about the possibility of arranging for someone to come live with his mother in Chicago. Unfortunately we did not get to make the plan before I left the country.

    I am in the business of lifting the human spirit to the next level, and would like to share another story with you before we close here. While I was dating Ayele the lady I just went to visit with her husband, I was in 10th grade and my high school band electric bass player had moved to another town and they needed someone who could replace him. Remy who was the lead guitar player encouraged me and gave me the confidence that I could play bass even though I told him that I could only play a little. He insisted that I could do it and I believed him and I became somewhat popular in the town as the youngest bass player the town ever had.

I later played at in the University band. Anyhow, Remy was now an unemployed musician with two teen-age children. As I went to see him, I asked about his brothers and sisters, he told me they all died of AIDS. He was the only one left and I noticed that they had a six-bedroom building in the middle of their compound with no roof on it whatsoever. I asked what the deal with the building with no roof was. He told me that his older brother had ordered the carpenters to take off the old roof so he could replace it with a new one but right after the roof was taken off, the older brother died of a heart attack. Now this nice building was just standing there as a financial opportunity missed. I asked him how munch it would cost to put a new roof and doors on the building and he told me about $500.00, so I told him that I did not have the money, but would manage to send him money once I returned to the U.S.

The deal was that I would help him fix the house and rent it out but he would have to collect the rent and send the money to my father so my father could complete the construction on my land. He was happy and grateful. Before I returned to the U.S., I made an arrangement with Tsphore to get Remy the money he needed for the roof and the doors.

CHAPTER FIFTEEN

I decided to go pay a visit to Appo, the gentleman who introduced me to the American Cultural Center in Africa. When I drove to Appo's house, the paint job on the house was the same except it was faded. I entered the house and asked to talk to Appo and was told he was absent. I came back another day and Appo was there and seemed to have lost a lot of weight. We gave each other a big hug and he could not believe that I would come all the way from the U.S. to visit him.

Appo was so proud and told his female cousins around the house that his friend came all the way from America to see him. Appo was eating breakfast when I got there so we went and sat in the living room to allow him to finish his food. Suddenly, Appo rushed to his bedroom and pulled out an old dusty wooden chest. He opened the chest and inside was this big beautiful sculpted ebony African traditional stool that he has commissioned a sculptor to make in 1986. This ebony stool had the bust of President Reagan carved in Ivory onto the middle piece and the Republican emblem onto each of its four corners.

There was also a sculpted ebony cane with the Republican emblem on it. Appo had wanted to give this stool, which is the representation of ultimate majesty in my culture, to President Reagan on his 75th birthday. Appo had gone to the American Embassy in Togo to talk to the people with the hope that they would help him send this magnificent gift to the President but was ignored by the people at the Embassy. Obviously Appo had hoped that if he could manage to get the gift to the President, maybe the President would be so moved that he would have been invited to come to America.

The people at the Embassy did not really care and they figured out Appo's intention. Appo was crushed. So he held onto the sculpture until today and this sculpture is one of his most valuable things in life at this point. He was proud to show it to me again. We talked about the past and I asked about his parents and he informed me that they both passed away and his brother who was a student at the University in the English Department.

Appo's brother supposedly joined some religious sect and got his brain "washed" and became a crazy man as he reported. As he ate his last scoop of food, he piled up about 15 different pills that he was going to take. He told me that thanks to those pills he was alive and I could see him at that point. I asked him what was going on with him and he said, "Tino, you know I am always frank with you. When you left, things got so bad that I had to get a job as an undertaker at the city morgue. I got AIDS by handling so many AIDS dead victims". I was shocked and sadden. I could almost guarantee that at the morgue the basic safety gear like rubber gloves for the undertaker were not there.

Appo said he did not know how long he was going to stay alive but he had hope. I felt I needed to do something to help him so I told him that I started an Internet business in America named GlobalMarketSales.com and that if he would sell me the sculptures, I would try to bring it with me to America and I would put them on auction on the site and hopefully some Republican would buy it and I would send him the cash difference between what I would pay him at that time. He replied that one of his uncles had offered him $1000.00 U.S. for it and he had declined it. He said he would need at least $5000.00 to be able to let it go.

That sculpture is everything he had and although he knew he was dying he said, it would take that amount of money to get him to part with the sculpture. I told him I did not have that money nor did I plan on spending that kind of money on the spot like that. He said it was okay. I felt very sorry for Appo, as I knew deep in my heart that if I did not get these sculptures from him soon, he would die of AIDS and his people would easily break it up to use as firewood. Appo gave me the copy of his blood test results with the hope that I would show them to some health care organization that would send him some medicine.

Somehow he hoped that I would show the picture of the sculpture to some organization in Alaska, which would send for him to go to Alaska. I gave Appo $200.00 and left and had hoped that it was not the last time I saw him. If you are out there and are interested in purchasing these beautiful sculptures and thus helping Appo, feel free to e-mail me at president@globalmarketsales.com. Hopefully by the time I receive your email, Appo would still be alive and I can make the necessary arrangement with you to get this timeless pieces.

    When I left Appo's place, I turned on the boulevard and saw this tall and beautiful young lady wearing denim jeans and a white T-shirt. I could tell that she must have been coming from a long trip because she had a big duffel bag over her shoulder. I passed her with the car and something hit me, I remember Suzie from Switzerland. I slowed down and I said hello, quickly introduced myself and offered to give her a ride. She looked at me, looked at the car, hesitated then she got into the car. I was wearing a T-shirt, a pair of shorts and my flip-flop sandals. Unless I told you, no one could ever guess that I was from America. As she got in the car, I reintroduced myself to her again and asked her name and how old she was. She said she was 20 and her name was Sabrina. I asked Sabrina where she was from and she said she was coming back from Benin. I asked her why she went to Benin, she replied that she went to visit her father who lived there and that she was kicked out of school for non-payment of the school fees. So she went to get the money from her father who had to work there because he could not find a job in Togo.

    As I asked if she had the money from her father to pay for the school fees, she said no and that her father told her that she would have to wait till the end of the following month. That whole conversation gave me a flash back to when I was in elementary school and the school principal would wait till we started the examinations and he would stop by each classroom and kick those who did not pay their school fees out. When the parents truly felt that their child would not have the opportunity to take the passing grade examination they would promptly manage to send the school fee. The school fee was about $2.00 back then but it was still a lot for people like my mother with 5 children to raise on an income from selling charcoal. I asked Sabrina which school she was going to and she said she was going to an accounting high school so she could become an accountant.

The Way It Was *Coming To America:* The Real Story.

I was very happy to hear that as I could see in her eyes the desire to become an accountant the way she said it. In fact school was important enough for her that she traveled all by herself all the way to the Republic of Benin to hope to get money to pay for it. I told her that I was from America visiting my family. I told her I am married with two children in America as to clearly make her at ease that I was not trying to hit on her.

When we got closer to her house, she made me drop her off about 500 feet from it. I did that because I did not want any of her relatives to think that there was a man in a Mercedes interested in their daughter. I just wanted to be an Angel for her. We setup an appointment to meet downtown Lomé so I could give her the money to pay for her school.

The next day we met, I took her to lunch and told her that she needed to stay focused on her education and to refrain from sexual activity or request that the boyfriend use condom. I told her that there would be plenty of time for all that and that she needed to make sure her future was taken care of first. I told her that I would try to help her if I could with her education. I asked if I could take some picture of her, and explained to her that I have published a web site called www.MissKwanzaa.com where I could post her picture if she wanted so that there would be a possibility that she could get a job as a model. I believe she has that natural African beauty that any marketer would love to use to promote a product targeted to the African American customer base.

If you are a marketer or need a picture of a naturally beautiful African young lady, please feel free to send your inquiry to president@globalmarketsales.com and I will communicate with you to see to it that we get a photo shoot for you. Sabrina could definitely use the money to help her parents with her own school fees. I am in the lifting of the human spirit business so please do not send me e-mail insinuating "Adult" intent with the story I just shared with you.

I truly want to be an Angel for more young people like Sabrina. Because you have bought this book, you might have already helped me reach another soul like Sabrina's. If you signup to become an affiliate for my company Global Market Sales Co. U.S.A., you too could join my team of the "Other people's Angels". Do you think you can be an Angel for someone?

The value of my current residence in America, when converted into the cfa currency is 80,000,000 francs cfa. If I sell 3 million copies of this book at the price of 19.95 each for example, we are looking at a total sale volume of $59,850,000.00 and America makes it possible; not by sitting and waiting for it to happen but rather by hard work and faith that one indeed can change one's circumstance if one is hungry for it. Ultimately one needs to have faith that God has given us all we need to succeed. I the child of the "lady who sells charcoal" they called her, am concluding this book with my heart pumping with confidence that I inspire you and encourage you to be grateful for everything you have.

We all have a story, you have read mine. People are willing to pay to hear your story. Logon to www.eibBooks.com to submit your story, I will personally review each story submitted. If your story warrants to be published, I will contact you directly and see to it the eibBooks.com gets it published and see that you are on "on your way" financially. But first you must make that first step: Logon to www.eibBooks.com to submit your story.

Thank you America, the land of the free. Free to be freaky or free to put in the "sweat" it takes to succeed! That is the question, that is the choice!!!!

The End.

eibBooks.com
As in Electronic Instant Books
As in eXcellence In Book Selling

Get your book published online instantly, electronically and/or in paperback format like this book and sell it directly on Zongo*Me*.com

We show you how!

The Way It Was *Coming To America:* The Real Story.

Grandma Añasee's house in my mother's village of Afagna. I lived here with my grandmother and my cousin until I moved to brother Andre and Etienne's house behind the church.

The Catholic church in the village of Afagna where I became a altar boy as an assurance that I will not miss church.

The Way It Was *Coming To America:* The Real Story.

Drums that we played in the church. On Sundays that I was not scheduled to serve as an altar boy, I joined the other children to play the drums to accompany the songs. I learned basic rhythmic music at this church.

My elementary Catholic school in Afagna where I attended 5th and 6th grade. My grandmother's neighborhood is right behind the school building. Under the trees is where the entrepreneur women sold students cooked meal for breakfast.

After graduating from elementary school in Afagna, I attended the Zebevi high-school in Aneho where I stayed with Uncle Gaspar. It was at this school where I was first introduced to English with Miss Sulton the American Peace Corp volunteer.

Our classroom at the high school. These desks were designed to sit two students but at times three to four students shared the desk.

The Way It Was *Coming To America:* The Real Story.

Ewe people's ancestral shrine in the village of Tado:

The lady with the white head wrap is the guardian of the Ewe-people ancestral shrine, here in the process of making a libation to the spirit of the ancestors with the request to bless the archaeological work this group of college student were going to perform in the village. Behind the lady is the actual shrine but one is forbidden to take picture of it.

The white circle is around Tino. Notice all the students had to take the shirts and shoes off in order to get close to the shrine. Everyone had to let go of any grudges and have nothing but positive thoughts. Failure to do so would result in the bees guarding the shrine attacking that individual.

It is at this shrine where Wayne the student from UCLA made his pledge to be accepted on his college basketball team and he got accepted as the shortest player ever to make the team in the college's history.

eibBooks.com
As in Electronic Instant Books
As in eXcellence In Book Selling

Get your book published online instantly, electronically and/or in paperback format like this book and sell it directly on Zongo*Me*.com

We show you how!

Movie Project.

eibBooks.com

The publisher of "The Way It Was Coming To America: The Real Story" plans to turn the story in this book into a movie distributed to the U.S. market and to the world market.

To submit your interest in participating in the movie production of this book, please mail your information to:

>eibBooks.com
>c/o Movie Project Department
>16781 Chagrin Blvd., Suite 255
>Shaker Heights OH, 44120

Make sure you provide your contact information, your daytime phone number and your email along with any expertise you have that may contribute to the project.

Be Other People's Angel

eibBooks.com

The publisher of "The Way It Was Coming To America: The Real Story" is sponsoring the publication of a collection of stories relating to people being an Angel to other people.

If you have a story that is worth reading because your action in its own way helps lift the human spirit on this earth, please submit that to our editorial department and you will be contacted as soon as possible. If your story has been selected to be included in the publication, the revenue of the sale of the book will be shared with you or with the charity of your choice.

Submit your story :

    eibBooks.com
    c/o Other People's Angel Dept.
    16781 Chagrin Blvd., Suite 255
    Shaker Heights OH, 44120

Make sure you provide your contact information, your daytime phone number and your email. You will be contacted by our editorial department.